GOD'S PLAN
FOR EVANGELISM AND DISCIPLESHIP

Holy Bible, New International Version
Matthew, Mark, Luke, John

Commentary by
CHUCK BROWN

Published by
CHUCK BROWN

GOD'S PLAN
FOR EVANGELISM AND DISCIPLESHIP

Copyright © 2016 by Chuck Brown
All Rights Reserved

Scripture taken from the Holy Bible, New International Version®, NIV®
Copyright © 1973, 1978, 1984, 2011 by Biblica, Inc.™
Used by permission of Zondervan. All rights reserved worldwide. WWW.ZONDERVAN.COM

The "NIV" and "New International Version" are trademarks registered in the United States Patent and Trademark Offices by Biblica, Inc.™

Table of Contents

PREFACE	i
CHRIST	1
AMBASSADOR	7
MISSION	13
PLAN	17
SECURITY	23
REWARD	29
HUMBLENESS	35
COMPASSION	41
LOVE	47
FORGIVENESS	53
MONEY	61
GUIDANCE	67
PROTECTION	71
SICKNESS	75
DEATH	81
DISOBEDIENCE	85
JUDGEMENT	91
WORKS	97
ETERNAL LIFE	103
INCARNATION	109
MIRACLES	115
ATONEMENT	121
RESURRECTION	127
ASCENSION	133
RETURN	137
COMMITMENT	143
REPENTANCE	149
FAITH	155
BAPTISM	161
PRAYER	165
COMMUNION	171
TEACHING	173
FELLOWSHIP—UNITY	177
FELLOWSHIP—POWER	181
FELLOWSHIP—STEWARDSHIP	183
REPRODUCTION—CALLING	189

REPRODUCTION—APPOINTMENT	195
REPRODUCTION—DELEGATION	199
REPRODUCTION—ACCOUNTABILITY	203
REPRODUCTION—INCREASE	205
GOSPEL PRESENTATION	209

PREFACE

What is God's plan? It is the principles that Jesus taught us in the bible. This book teaches these principles in a systematic way so that it is easier to see the plan and obey it. This book is based upon the Gospels: Matthew, Mark, Luke, and John. I limited the book to these gospels because I believe that in them Jesus taught all that was needed to begin and grow the Christian church.

What motivated me to write this book? I believe that God still works through his Ambassadors today, even performing miracles as needed, for Ambassadors who remain in him and are working his plan.

John 15:4-5 (NIV)

[4] Remain in me, as I also remain in you. No branch can bear fruit by itself; it must remain in the vine. Neither can you bear fruit unless you remain in me.

[5] "I am the vine; you are the branches. If you remain in me and I in you, you will bear much fruit; apart from me you can do nothing.

I asked myself, "What does it mean to remain in him?" And do the gospels lay out a plan to remain in him? I determined to read the gospels until I found the plan. I had a three ring binder which had separators for each category of scripture and I began categorizing scriptures into these categories until I found an outline of the plan, then for each outline item I made sure that the scriptures related to that outline item. In deciding which scriptures to include in the book I determined to let the preponderance of the evidence to decide that. If there were multiple scriptures that said the same thing then I selected the one that said it best. When deciding when to use a scripture I let the theme or direction of the scriptures to decide when to use them so that there was a natural fit. For each scripture used in this book I wrote a commentary according to the way I see God's plan for God's Ambassadors. So this book was researched, designed, and written in a systematic way. I feel very confident that this book is God's plan because of the comprehensive and systematic way it was written. So in a systematic way the book, God's plan, shows how to reach out to unbelievers, and once saved to disciple them until they become mature Ambassadors who then reach out to more unbelievers and duplicate this process over and over again in order to grow the church.

CHRIST

Jesus is the king of the Jews. He is also king of his Ambassadors.

One of the reasons that the Jews did not accept Jesus as their king is because they expected the Christ to be a conquering king, who would free them from Roman rule. Jesus did not come as a conquering Messiah as they expected, he came as a humble servant who taught and preached a message of repentance and faith, and performed many miracles. His disciples observed the miracles and believed and accepted him as their king, someone to be followed and obeyed. They believed that Jesus knew, taught, and lived God's plan for having eternal life. They, in the beginning, did not understand that Jesus would have to die to fulfill God's plan to make eternal life a reality.

The good news is that Jesus died and made eternal life a reality and that he made it a possibility for everyone who has ever lived. There is a condition for entering eternal life, and that condition is that one must have put their faith in Jesus as Savior and Lord.

John 3:16 (NIV)

[16] For God so loved the world that he gave his one and only Son, that whoever believes in him shall not perish but have eternal life.

The bible is clear about Jesus being the king, Christ, Messiah, and Son of God. Today's Ambassadors should obey and follow Jesus as he taught and lived according to God's plan.

Jesus declared to the Samaritan woman whom he met at the well that he was the Messiah and Christ that everyone had been waiting for. He explained God's plan to the Samaritan's for entering eternal life and many became believers.

☦ GOD'S PLAN FOR EVANGELISM AND DISCIPLESHIP ☦

John 4:25-26 (NIV)

²⁵ The woman said, "I know that Messiah" (called Christ) "is coming. When he comes, he will explain everything to us."

²⁶ Then Jesus declared, "I, the one speaking to you—I am he."

John 4:39-41 (NIV)

³⁹ Many of the Samaritans from that town believed in him because of the woman's testimony, "He told me everything I ever did." ⁴⁰ So when the Samaritans came to him, they urged him to stay with them, and he stayed two days. ⁴¹ And because of his words many more became believers.

Jesus declared to the Jewish leaders that he was the Christ, Son of Man, and Son of God, but they did not believe him.

Luke 22:66-71 (NIV)

⁶⁶ At daybreak the council of the elders of the people, both the chief priests and the teachers of the law, met together, and Jesus was led before them. ⁶⁷ "If you are the Messiah," they said, "tell us."

Jesus answered, "If I tell you, you will not believe me, ⁶⁸ and if I asked you, you would not answer. ⁶⁹ But from now on, the Son of Man will be seated at the right hand of the mighty God."

⁷⁰ They all asked, "Are you then the Son of God?"

He replied, "You say that I am."

⁷¹ Then they said, "Why do we need any more testimony? We have heard it from his own lips."

Jesus declared to Pilate, the governor, that he was the king of the Jews, and that his kingdom was from another world. He said that he came into the world to testify to the truth of God's plan.

Luke 23:1-3 (NIV)

[1] Then the whole assembly rose and led him off to Pilate. [2] And they began to accuse him, saying, "We have found this man subverting our nation. He opposes payment of taxes to Caesar and claims to be Messiah, a king."

[3] So Pilate asked Jesus, "Are you the king of the Jews?"

"You have said so," Jesus replied.

John 18:36-37 (NIV)

[36] Jesus said, "My kingdom is not of this world. If it were, my servants would fight to prevent my arrest by the Jewish leaders. But now my kingdom is from another place."

[37] "You are a king, then!" said Pilate.

Jesus answered, "You say that I am a king. In fact, the reason I was born and came into the world is to testify to the truth. Everyone on the side of truth listens to me."

Jesus demonstrated that he was the sovereign king by using his authority and power over creation; for example, nature, demons, sickness, and death including his own resurrection.

An example of Jesus' authority over nature is when he commanded the waves, in a furious storm, to be still and they obeyed him.

✞ GOD'S PLAN FOR EVANGELISM AND DISCIPLESHIP ✞

Matthew 8:23-27 (NIV)

²³ Then he got into the boat and his disciples followed him. ²⁴ Suddenly a furious storm came up on the lake, so that the waves swept over the boat. But Jesus was sleeping. ²⁵ The disciples went and woke him, saying, "Lord, save us! We're going to drown!"

²⁶ He replied, "You of little faith, why are you so afraid?" Then he got up and rebuked the winds and the waves, and it was completely calm.

²⁷ The men were amazed and asked, "What kind of man is this? Even the winds and the waves obey him!"

An example of Jesus' authority over demons is when he rebuked them and cast them out. The demons obeyed his command because they knew that he was the Christ and Son of God and had the authority to do so.

Luke 4:41 (NIV)

⁴¹ Moreover, demons came out of many people, shouting, "You are the Son of God!" But he rebuked them and would not allow them to speak, because they knew he was the Messiah.

An example of Jesus' authority over sickness is when he touched a person with a fever and that fever left her.

Matthew 8:14-15 (NIV)

¹⁴ When Jesus came into Peter's house, he saw Peter's mother-in-law lying in bed with a fever. ¹⁵ He touched her hand and the fever left her, and she got up and began to wait on him.

An example of Jesus' authority over death is when he was able to release his spirit and die and be resurrected by his own authority and timing. Ordinary men do not have this authority.

Luke 23:46-49 (NIV)

[46] Jesus called out with a loud voice, "Father, into your hands I commit my spirit."[a] When he had said this, he breathed his last.

[47] The centurion, seeing what had happened, praised God and said, "Surely this was a righteous man." [48] When all the people who had gathered to witness this sight saw what took place, they beat their breasts and went away. [49] But all those who knew him, including the women who had followed him from Galilee, stood at a distance, watching these things.

John 2:18-21 (NIV)

[18] The Jews then responded to him, "What sign can you show us to prove your authority to do all this?"

[19] Jesus answered them, "Destroy this temple, and I will raise it again in three days." [20] They replied, "It has taken forty-six years to build this temple, and you are going to raise it in three days?" [21] But the temple he had spoken of was his body.

✟ GOD'S PLAN FOR EVANGELISM AND DISCIPLESHIP ✟

DISCUSSION QUESTIONS

1. Why did the Jews not believe that Jesus was the Christ?
2. Why did the disciples believe that Jesus was the Christ?
3. In the beginning, what was it that the disciples did not understand about Jesus?
4. What kind of relationship should Ambassadors have with Jesus?
5. What was it that made the Samaritans believe that Jesus was the Christ?
6. Where did Jesus say that his kingdom was from?
7. How did Jesus demonstrate that he had authority over all creation?
8. Why did the Jewish leaders want to take Jesus to Pilate?
9. What did we learn about Jesus' kingship from this category?

AMBASSADOR

Ambassador – a diplomatic official of the highest rank, sent by one sovereign or state to another as its resident representative.

Jesus is the king of heaven who was sent by the Father to establish his church in the world.

John 8:42 (NIV)

42 Jesus said to them, "If God were your Father, you would love me, for I have come here from God. I have not come on my own; God sent me."

And Jesus also said that he was sent by God the Father with God's plan to obey.

John 12:49 (NIV)

49 For I did not speak on my own, but the Father who sent me commanded me to say all that I have spoken.

Jesus obeyed God's plan during his ministry here on earth then returned to his home in heaven.

John 7:33-34 (NIV)

33 Jesus said, "I am with you for only a short time, and then I am going to the one who sent me. 34 You will look for me, but you will not find me; and where I am, you cannot come."

Once you accept Jesus as Lord and Savior you become a Christian Ambassador; and Christian Ambassadors trust and obey the will of God: God's plan.

Jesus is the king of kings and Christians are his Ambassadors. Jesus trained twelve of his closest disciples and then sent them

✝ GOD'S PLAN FOR EVANGELISM AND DISCIPLESHIP ✝

out into the world to be his Ambassadors. Just as citizens in this world's kingdoms are to obey their king, Christian Ambassadors are to go into the world and obey Jesus as their king.

John 17:18 (NIV)

18 As you sent me into the world, I have sent them into the world.

John 20:21 (NIV)

21 Again Jesus said, "Peace be with you! As the Father has sent me, I am sending you."

Jesus talked about a paradigm shift where the old religious plan of Judaism was to be replaced with a new plan. Judaism had its own plan to get to heaven which included following all its rules and traditions. God's plan was the new plan to get to heaven which included putting one's faith in Jesus as Savior and Lord. Jesus established this new plan and then Jesus's followers were to continue implementing this new plan after Jesus's death, resurrection, and ascension to heaven. Jesus told his Ambassadors to wait until the day of Pentecost when the Holy Spirit would come upon them in power so they could start the new church with the new plan.

Jesus did not come to fix Judaism, the old garment. No, he came to establish a new plan, the new garment, so that he could pour new wine, the Holy Spirit, into the new church.

Mark 2:21-22 (NIV)

21 "No one sews a patch of unshrunk cloth on an old garment. Otherwise, the new piece will pull away from the old, making the tear worse. 22 And no one pours new wine into old wineskins. Otherwise, the wine will burst the skins, and both

the wine and the wineskins will be ruined. No, they pour new wine into new wineskins."

The new Christian should be taught about how to perceive the world from the new Christian Ambassador's perspective. And what is that perspective? In short, it's realizing that their eternal home headquarters is in heaven, their temporal residence is where they live in this world, and their enemy is Satan, who tries to thwart Ambassadors from obeying God's plan. Their mission is to warn unbelievers that their eternal destiny is hell unless they put their faith in Jesus. And Christians are to have a relationship with Jesus as a king has with his Ambassadors. Churches are to function as embassies to the world. Churches are places of business where disciples are to learn how to function as Ambassadors to the world. Once an Ambassador has made the paradigm shift in their minds they can more easily understand God's plan and act as God's Ambassadors with power.

Included in this perspective is that Satan, demons, and angels are real. Satan is the prince of this world who uses temptation to distract people from following God's plan. He tempted Jesus in three areas and Jesus persevered over those temptations by holding on to God's word. And after those temptations angels came and attended to him. One of Satan's biggest temptations is with materialism or with the love of money. When he tempted Jesus with materialism, Jesus answered that we should worship God and serve him only. We too are tempted with the love of money to the point where we lose our faith in God to provide for us. We live as though God doesn't provide and that we must provide for ourselves. God does provide and says that if we seek him first he will provide all of our material needs.

Matthew 4:1-11 (NIV)

[1] Then Jesus was led by the Spirit into the wilderness to be tempted[a] by the devil. [2] After fasting forty days and forty

nights, he was hungry. ³ The tempter came to him and said, "If you are the Son of God, tell these stones to become bread."

⁴ Jesus answered, "It is written: 'Man shall not live on bread alone, but on every word that comes from the mouth of God.'[b]"

⁵ Then the devil took him to the holy city and had him stand on the highest point of the temple. ⁶ "If you are the Son of God," he said, "throw yourself down. For it is written:

"'He will command his angels concerning you,
 and they will lift you up in their hands,
 so that you will not strike your foot against a stone.'[c]"

⁷ Jesus answered him, "It is also written: 'Do not put the Lord your God to the test.'[d]"

⁸ Again, the devil took him to a very high mountain and showed him all the kingdoms of the world and their splendor. ⁹ "All this I will give you," he said, "if you will bow down and worship me."

¹⁰ Jesus said to him, "Away from me, Satan! For it is written: 'Worship the Lord your God, and serve him only.'[e]"

¹¹ Then the devil left him, and angels came and attended him.

Matthew 6:31-33 (NIV)

³¹ So do not worry, saying, 'What shall we eat?' or 'What shall we drink?' or 'What shall we wear?' ³² For the pagans run after all these things, and your heavenly Father knows that you need them. ³³ But seek first his kingdom and his righteousness, and all these things will be given to you as well.

When Jesus called his first disciples he got their attention by meeting their financial needs in a miraculous way. These disciples learned that they could trust Jesus with their financial needs so that is why they felt confident they could leave their fishing businesses to join Jesus in becoming fishers of men.

Luke 5:1-11 (NIV)

¹ One day as Jesus was standing by the Lake of Gennesaret,[a] the people were crowding around him and listening to the word of God. ² He saw at the water's edge two boats, left there by the fishermen, who were washing their nets. ³ He got into one of the boats, the one belonging to Simon, and asked him to put out a little from shore. Then he sat down and taught the people from the boat.

⁴ When he had finished speaking, he said to Simon, "Put out into deep water, and let down the nets for a catch."

⁵ Simon answered, "Master, we've worked hard all night and haven't caught anything. But because you say so, I will let down the nets."

⁶ When they had done so, they caught such a large number of fish that their nets began to break. ⁷ So they signaled their partners in the other boat to come and help them, and they came and filled both boats so full that they began to sink.

⁸ When Simon Peter saw this, he fell at Jesus' knees and said, "Go away from me, Lord; I am a sinful man!" ⁹ For he and all his companions were astonished at the catch of fish they had taken, ¹⁰ and so were James and John, the sons of Zebedee, Simon's partners.

Then Jesus said to Simon, "Don't be afraid; from now on you will fish for people." ¹¹ So they pulled their boats up on shore, left everything and followed him.

✟ GOD'S PLAN FOR EVANGELISM AND DISCIPLESHIP ✟

DISCUSSION QUESTIONS

1. What are Ambassadors?
2. How was Jesus an Ambassador?
3. How were the disciples Ambassadors of Christ?
4. Why was Judaism considered the old garment in the parable?
5. Why was the new church considered the new garment in the parable?
6. How are today's Ambassadors to live according to Christ's Ambassador perspective?
7. Why were the disciples willing to leave their fishing business to follow Jesus?

MISSION

Every person has been created by God and God has a mission for every person. Some accept God's grace and learn and obey the mission, these are Christians. Others never accept the grace or learn or obey the mission, these are non-Christians. This book explains what that mission is and God's plan for sharing that mission.

Jesus said that his mission was to preach the good news of the kingdom of God.

Luke 4:43 (NIV)

[43] But he said, "I must proclaim the good news of the kingdom of God to the other towns also, because that is why I was sent."

He preached the good news to a mostly Jewish audience that was looking forward to the coming of the Messiah who would establish an earthly kingdom and be a conquering king who would free them from Roman rule and oppression. But that is not the kind of kingdom he came to establish so many of the Jews did not accept him as the Messiah.

Jesus was sent by God to preach the good news of the kingdom of God. The good news is that the Messiah has come to provide salvation for his disciples so that they could experience eternal life with him. He came to establish and grow his kingdom here on earth; and to teach his Ambassadors how to follow God's plan. His disciples did not understand that he had to die for their sins, be resurrected, and ascend to heaven as a part of God's plan,

He came preaching a message of repentance.

✞ GOD'S PLAN FOR EVANGELISM AND DISCIPLESHIP ✞

Matthew 4:17 (NIV)

¹⁷ From that time on Jesus began to preach, "Repent, for the kingdom of heaven has come near."

Jesus wanted people to stop thinking and behaving in a self-centered manner. He wanted people to stop living according their own plan and to start living according to God's plan. The kingdom of God is near because time is running out before Jesus returns in judgment. Jesus has already come, during his first coming, and did all that was needed to break the bondage to sin and make it possible to live in freedom with God. With the mission of the first coming accomplished, the mission of the second coming is near. This is an urgent message because although salvation is free offer, it is also a limited time offer. People need to accept Jesus as their savior and king before his second coming or before they die in their sins; otherwise, they will have an eternity in hell waiting for them as their destiny after judgment. While if they accept Jesus as their savior and king, their eternal destiny is in heaven after judgment. There is a choice to be made and it is a choice that must be made before you die or Jesus returns, whichever comes first.

Jesus' mission had three facets to it: preaching, teaching, and healing. He preached the urgent message that the kingdom of God was near, he taught God's plan in the synagogues, and he healed those needing healing of various ailments. His healing authenticated his preaching and teaching messages, that he was the Messiah who was sent by God to save his people.

Matthew 4:23 (NIV)

²³ Jesus went throughout Galilee, teaching in their synagogues, proclaiming the good news of the kingdom, and healing every disease and sickness among the people.

Jesus sent his twelve apostles, the first kingdom Ambassadors, with the mission of preaching the same urgent message that John the Baptist preached and Jesus preached earlier; that people need to repent because the kingdom of God was near. And he gave his Ambassadors the power to heal so that the people would know that they too were sent by God to save his people through Jesus the Messiah.

Matthew 10:7-8 (NIV)

[7] As you go, proclaim this message: 'The kingdom of heaven has come near.' [8] Heal the sick, raise the dead, cleanse those who have leprosy,[a] drive out demons. Freely you have received; freely give.

Jesus' final mission to his Ambassadors, called the Great Commission, was to make disciples of all nations teaching them God's plan, which went beyond preaching and healing; it included everything that Jesus had taught them, which later was written in the four gospels: Matthew, Mark, Luke, and John. This book, God's Plan is based upon what is taught in those four gospels. I believe that Jesus taught all that was needed to get the kingdom founded and growing. After Jesus ascended into heaven he sent his Holy Spirit to help his Ambassadors to spread the message with power.

Matthew 28:19-20 (NIV)

[19] Therefore go and make disciples of all nations, baptizing them in the name of the Father and of the Son and of the Holy Spirit, [20] and teaching them to obey everything I have commanded you. And surely I am with you always, to the very end of the age."

✟ GOD'S PLAN FOR EVANGELISM AND DISCIPLESHIP ✟

DISCUSSION QUESTIONS

1. What is the good news of the kingdom of God?
2. What does it mean to repent?
3. What did healing do for the other two facets?
4. What was the first mission that Jesus sent his twelve apostles to perform?
5. What was the final mission that Jesus sent his twelve apostles to perform?

PLAN

Jesus is the personification of God's plan because he lived perfectly according to God's plan. He said that he is the way, the truth, the life, and the only way to the Father.

John 14:2-6 (NIV)

2 My Father's house has many rooms; if that were not so, would I have told you that I am going there to prepare a place for you? 3 And if I go and prepare a place for you, I will come back and take you to be with me that you also may be where I am. 4 You know the way to the place where I am going."

5 Thomas said to him, "Lord, we don't know where you are going, so how can we know the way?"

6 Jesus answered, "I am the way and the truth and the life. No one comes to the Father except through me.

Thomas asked Jesus the question that many disciples ask. How do we get to the Father's house in heaven? What is the plan? The plan is to receive Jesus as savior, then to follow and obey him as Lord because he is the only way to the Father's house in heaven. Heaven is the place where Ambassadors go to after their work on earth has ended. They leave their temporary residences on earth to go to their eternal homes in heaven. If we want to know what to do to get there, then follow Jesus as your role model. Know the words and works of Jesus and try to do the same. This book tries to teach the words and works of Jesus in a systematic way so that God's plan may be seen more clearly.

✟ GOD'S PLAN FOR EVANGELISM AND DISCIPLESHIP ✟

John 8:12 (NIV)

¹² When Jesus spoke again to the people, he said, "I am the light of the world. Whoever follows me will never walk in darkness, but will have the light of life."

Jesus leads people out of the darkness and into the light by opening their eyes to the truth of God's word. The world is a dark place, but Ambassadors have been given Jesus who is the light. He shows Ambassadors how to walk in the light of God's word. Because Jesus obeyed God's plan perfectly he is the personification of God's light. Ambassadors should get to know their bible inside and out so that they can clearly see the plan. Today, Ambassadors have the Holy Spirit to be their light who reveals God's plan to them so that they can follow Jesus as Lord. The Holy Spirit reminds us of the words and works of Jesus that are recorded in the bible.

John 3:19-21 (NIV)

¹⁹ This is the verdict: Light has come into the world, but people loved darkness instead of light because their deeds were evil. ²⁰ Everyone who does evil hates the light, and will not come into the light for fear that their deeds will be exposed. ²¹ But whoever lives by the truth comes into the light, so that it may be seen plainly that what they have done has been done in the sight of God.

People have a choice. Just as Adam and Eve had a choice; they could have obeyed God or Satan. One choice leads to life and the other leads to death. One leads to light and the other to darkness. One pleases God and the other self and Satan. One satisfies the cravings of the new nature and the other the old sin nature. People who disobey God try to run and hide from God in fear of his disapproval because they do not like to have their guilt and sin exposed. Ambassadors who obey God do their obedience in the open so they can receive God's approval and praise. People who obey God have God's help in achieving God's plan. Satan does not want people to achieve God's plan. Satan tempts everyone to do anything but God's plan. The Christian lifestyle should be such that people acknowledge that what was done has been done through God, and non-Christians should take notice and ask where Christians got this way of living, and Christians should be prepared to give an answer to them. The Christian lifestyle should be attractive to non-Christians who are seeking after God. Christians are to live lives of righteousness by yielding to the Holy Spirit who works in them and through them.

Matthew 7:13-14 (NIV)

[13] "Enter through the narrow gate. For wide is the gate and broad is the road that leads to destruction, and many enter through it. [14] But small is the gate and narrow the road that leads to life, and only a few find it."

The road to God's house is narrow because, as Jesus said, he was the only way to the father The road to Satan's house is wide because it includes any and all ways but God's way. Only a few find God's way because many are blinded by sin from seeing it. Man's spiritual eyes have been blinded to the truth because of sin. The only way to overcome this sin is through salvation. Ambassadors have been saved and their eyes have been opened to be able to see the truth. Ambassadors are to seek the spiritually blind and share God's plan with them.

Jesus said that Ambassadors would sometimes experience times of trials and tribulation and he told the following parable about it.

Matthew 7:24-27 (NIV)

[24] "Therefore, everyone who hears these words of mine and puts them into practice is like a wise man who built his house

on the rock. ²⁵ The rain came down, the streams rose, and the winds blew and beat against that house; yet it did not fall, because it had its foundation on the rock. ²⁶ But everyone who hears these words of mine and does not put them into practice is like a foolish man who built his house on sand. ²⁷ The rain came down, the streams rose, and the winds blew and beat against that house, and it fell with a great crash."

When times of trials and tribulation come those who persist in following God's plan will stand in victory, but those who do not will fall in defeat. Get the support of other Ambassadors to help and advise you on how to make it through these times. Satan wants us to fail and give up, but God wants us to withstand the trouble and have victory.

Matthew 11:28-30 (NIV)

²⁸ "Come to me, all you who are weary and burdened, and I will give you rest. ²⁹ Take my yoke upon you and learn from me, for I am gentle and humble in heart, and you will find rest for your souls. ³⁰ For my yoke is easy and my burden is light."

Learn God's plan because while you are doing it you can rest assured that God is on your side giving you a rest that only he can give. This is a benefit that affects your entire being.

Taking on God's yoke or God's plan also brings with it the fruit of the Holy Spirit which is love, joy, peace, patience, kindness, goodness, faithfulness, gentleness and self-control. Anyone seeking after these benefits or fruits should accept Jesus as his Savior and began to follow him as Lord by obeying God's plan.

DISCUSSION QUESTIONS

1. Why is Jesus considered the personification of God's plan?
2. Why did Jesus say that he was the light of the world?
3. Why is the narrow gate considered God's plan?
4. Why is the broad gate considered Satan's plan?

✝ GOD'S PLAN FOR EVANGELISM AND DISCIPLESHIP ✝

SECURITY

God wants Ambassadors to trust him to meet their temporal needs. As Ambassadors trust and obey God's plan, he promises to provide the financial resources that we need for things like food and clothing. God does not wants Ambassadors to worry about whether they are making or have accumulated enough money and material goods, for God knows our financial needs and will supply them on a just in time basis. The money and material goods belong to God and he wants Ambassadors to be good stewards of these things. Unbelievers believe that the money and material goods belong to them and that they should try to make and accumulate as much as they can so that they can retire with a feeling of financial security. However, money and material goods are here today and gone tomorrow and cannot be trusted to bring financial security. God is our security. We are to do the work of Ambassadors and not worry about chasing after money. He wants Ambassadors to put their faith in Him alone for our financial security. Jesus does not want his Ambassadors to have doubts or "little faith" in believing that God would provide for them.

Matthew 6:19-34 (NIV)

[19] "Do not store up for yourselves treasures on earth, where moths and vermin destroy, and where thieves break in and steal. [20] But store up for yourselves treasures in heaven, where moths and vermin do not destroy, and where thieves do not break in and steal. [21] For where your treasure is, there your heart will be also.

[22] "The eye is the lamp of the body. If your eyes are healthy,[a] your whole body will be full of light. [23] But if your eyes are unhealthy,[b] your whole body will be full of darkness. If then the light within you is darkness, how great is that darkness!

24 "No one can serve two masters. Either you will hate the one and love the other, or you will be devoted to the one and despise the other. You cannot serve both God and money.

25 "Therefore I tell you, do not worry about your life, what you will eat or drink; or about your body, what you will wear. Is not life more than food, and the body more than clothes? 26 Look at the birds of the air; they do not sow or reap or store away in barns, and yet your heavenly Father feeds them. Are you not much more valuable than they? 27 Can any one of you by worrying add a single hour to your life[c]?

28 "And why do you worry about clothes? See how the flowers of the field grow. They do not labor or spin. 29 Yet I tell you that not even Solomon in all his splendor was dressed like one of these. 30 If that is how God clothes the grass of the field, which is here today and tomorrow is thrown into the fire, will he not much more clothe you—you of little faith? 31 So do not worry, saying, 'What shall we eat?' or 'What shall we drink?' or 'What shall we wear?' 32 For the pagans run after all these things, and your heavenly Father knows that you need them. 33 But seek first his kingdom and his righteousness, and all these things will be given to you as well. 34 Therefore do not worry about tomorrow, for tomorrow will worry about itself. Each day has enough trouble of its own.

Luke 12:22-24 (NIV)

22 Then Jesus said to his disciples: "Therefore I tell you, do not worry about your life, what you will eat; or about your body, what you will wear. 23 For life is more than food, and the body more than clothes. 24 Consider the ravens: They do not sow or reap, they have no storeroom or barn; yet God feeds them. And how much more valuable you are than birds!

Jesus tells a story of a rich man who had a big harvest and decided that his barns were not big enough to contain it all so he decided to tear down his barns and build bigger ones so that he could retire: take life easy; eat, drink and be merry. In God's kingdom there is no retirement. Money and material wealth are not to be stored up for the purpose of resting and living in retirement. Every day that God gives us is to be used to serve him by obeying God's plan.

Luke 12:16-21 (NIV)

[16] And he told them this parable: "The ground of a certain rich man yielded an abundant harvest. [17] He thought to himself, 'What shall I do? I have no place to store my crops.'

[18] "Then he said, 'This is what I'll do. I will tear down my barns and build bigger ones, and there I will store my surplus grain. [19] And I'll say to myself, "You have plenty of grain laid up for many years. Take life easy; eat, drink and be merry."'

[20] "But God said to him, 'You fool! This very night your life will be demanded from you. Then who will get what you have prepared for yourself?'

[21] "This is how it will be with whoever stores up things for themselves but is not rich toward God."

The usual way that God provided money for Jesus and his Ambassadors was through paying them for their teaching and preaching in the synagogues based on the principle "the worker is worth his keep"

Matthew 10:5-16 (NIV)

[5] These twelve Jesus sent out with the following instructions: "Do not go among the Gentiles or enter any town of the Samaritans. [6] Go rather to the lost sheep of Israel. [7] As you go, proclaim this message: 'The kingdom of heaven has come near.' [8] Heal the sick, raise the dead, cleanse those who have

✟ GOD'S PLAN FOR EVANGELISM AND DISCIPLESHIP ✟

leprosy,[a] drive out demons. Freely you have received; freely give.

⁹ "Do not get any gold or silver or copper to take with you in your belts— ¹⁰ no bag for the journey or extra shirt or sandals or a staff, for the worker is worth his keep. ¹¹ Whatever town or village you enter, search there for some worthy person and stay at their house until you leave. ¹² As you enter the home, give it your greeting. ¹³ If the home is deserving, let your peace rest on it; if it is not, let your peace return to you. ¹⁴ If anyone will not welcome you or listen to your words, leave that home or town and shake the dust off your feet. ¹⁵ Truly I tell you, it will be more bearable for Sodom and Gomorrah on the Day of Judgment than for that town.

¹⁶ "I am sending you out like sheep among wolves. Therefore, be as shrewd as snakes and as innocent as doves.

Luke 10:1-7 (NIV)

¹ After this the Lord appointed seventy-two[a] others and sent them two by two ahead of him to every town and place where he was about to go. ² He told them, "The harvest is plentiful, but the workers are few. Ask the Lord of the harvest, therefore, to send out workers into his harvest field. ³ Go! I am sending you out like lambs among wolves. ⁴ Do not take a purse or bag or sandals; and do not greet anyone on the road.

⁵ "When you enter a house, first say, 'Peace to this house.' ⁶ If someone who promotes peace is there, your peace will rest on them; if not, it will return to you. ⁷ Stay there, eating and drinking whatever they give you, for the worker deserves his wages. Do not move around from house to house.

A synagogue had somewhere near ten or more families in them. The ruling elder of the synagogue would find a traveling rabbi to teach on the Sabbath. The elder and rabbis were paid for their services by the tithe and offerings from the families they served in the synagogue.

Ambassadors have their security in God. As they work God's plan, God provides for their daily needs. God's provision usually comes from the people who benefit from the Ambassador's teaching. As the Ambassador's number of disciples increases the amount of their income increases, particularly when their disciples become Ambassadors in their own right. These income resources add more money for sowing and reaping so the Ambassador can be even more fruitful. Ambassadors need not worry about their provision, as the scripture says, "seek first his kingdom and his righteousness, and all these things will be given to you as well" "All these things" are the daily needs that God provides. So by working God's plan Ambassadors are compensated by God in whom they have their security.

✠ GOD'S PLAN FOR EVANGELISM AND DISCIPLESHIP ✠

DISCUSSION QUESTIONS

1. To whom does money and material goods belong?
2. What is the purpose of money and material goods from the Ambassador's perspective?
3. What is the purpose of money and material goods from the unbeliever's perspective?
4. Financial security comes from doing what?
5. When does retirement begin?
6. Under what principle did Jesus and his Ambassadors get paid for working God's plan?

REWARD

Heavenly rewards are given by Jesus to Ambassadors at the judgment for service they have performed on earth. Rewards are earned. By contrast, salvation is a gift and cannot be earned.

Matthew 16:27 (NIV)

27 For the Son of Man is going to come in his Father's glory with his angels, and then he will reward each person according to what they have done.

Jesus said an Ambassador can earn rewards for various acts done for other Ambassadors. These do not have to be big or complex deeds, they can be very simple deeds. Jesus said that for receiving a prophet or a righteous man you will get a prophet's or a righteous man's reward and that is an incentive for helping God's people. God wants us to care for and help each other; which builds bonds of fellowship. When non-believers see the way Ambassadors care for each other then they may want to become Ambassadors too.

Matthew 10:40-42 (NIV)

40 "Anyone who welcomes you welcomes me, and anyone who welcomes me welcomes the one who sent me. 41 Whoever welcomes a prophet as a prophet will receive a prophet's reward, and whoever welcomes a righteous person as a righteous person will receive a righteous person's reward. 42 And if anyone gives even a cup of cold water to one of these little ones who is my disciple, truly I tell you, that person will certainly not lose their reward."

Jesus will give us heavenly rewards for loving our enemies too. Most people are willing to do good for those who do good for them, but not do the same for those who do evil things to them.

Ambassadors must be different and will be rewarded for being different. Ambassadors should be willing to do good to both fellow Ambassadors and the lost and so to be perfect as their heavenly Father is perfect

Matthew 5:43-48 (NIV)

⁴³ "You have heard that it was said, 'Love your neighbor[a] and hate your enemy.' ⁴⁴ But I tell you, love your enemies and pray for those who persecute you, ⁴⁵ that you may be children of your Father in heaven. He causes his sun to rise on the evil and the good, and sends rain on the righteous and the unrighteous. ⁴⁶ If you love those who love you, what reward will you get? Are not even the tax collectors doing that? ⁴⁷ And if you greet only your own people, what are you doing more than others? Do not even pagans do that? ⁴⁸ Be perfect, therefore, as your heavenly Father is perfect."

Jesus will give us heavenly rewards for helping people from our wealth. It's not our wealth, it is God's wealth, and we are stewards of his wealth. Jesus wants us to be willing to sell our possessions in order to give to the needy. How we spend God's wealth says where our heart is. Wealth is temporal and is lost as soon as it is found. Thieves break in and steal it and it gets used up on selfish desires, we get heavenly rewards for using it for others for the building up of the kingdom of God.

Luke 12:33-34 (NIV)

³³ Sell your possessions and give to the poor. Provide purses for yourselves that will not wear out, a treasure in heaven that will never fail, where no thief comes near and no moth destroys. ³⁴ For where your treasure is, there your heart will be also.

Jesus will give us heavenly rewards for not excluding the poor, the crippled, the lame, and the blind. It is easy to provide a service for those who have provided for us and can repay us later. Jesus wants us to give to those who will not be able to repay us in this life.

Luke 14:12-14 (NIV)

[12] Then Jesus said to his host, "When you give a luncheon or dinner, do not invite your friends, your brothers or sisters, your relatives, or your rich neighbors; if you do, they may invite you back and so you will be repaid. [13] But when you give a banquet, invite the poor, the crippled, the lame, the blind, [14] and you will be blessed. Although they cannot repay you, you will be repaid at the resurrection of the righteous."

Jesus will give us heavenly rewards for doing our good deeds in private. In fact, if you do your good deeds to be noticed by the public you will not get a heavenly reward, because you would have already received your temporal reward in full. That temporal reward may be in the form of praises or prizes that man gives to us.

Matthew 6:1-4 (NIV)

[1] "Be careful not to practice your righteousness in front of others to be seen by them. If you do, you will have no reward from your Father in heaven.

[2] "So when you give to the needy, do not announce it with trumpets, as the hypocrites do in the synagogues and on the streets, to be honored by others. Truly I tell you, they have received their reward in full. [3] But when you give to the needy, do not let your left hand know what your right hand is doing, [4] so that your giving may be in secret. Then your Father, who sees what is done in secret, will reward you."

Jesus will give us heavenly rewards for fasting in private. Jesus does not want us to look somber or disheveled when we are fasting. If we do then we will not get a reward in heaven because we will have already received a temporal reward in full from man. So Jesus says that we should prepare our appearance so that people do not know that we are fasting.

Matthew 6:16-18 (NIV)

[16] "When you fast, do not look somber as the hypocrites do, for they disfigure their faces to show others they are fasting. Truly I tell you, they have received their reward in full. [17] But when you fast, put oil on your head and wash your face, [18] so that it will not be obvious to others that you are fasting, but only to your Father, who is unseen; and your Father, who sees what is done in secret, will reward you."

Jesus will give us heavenly rewards for enduring persecution. Ambassadors should be ready and willing to endure persecution for Christ because that is the same way that the prophets before us were treated. Ambassadors will be hated, excluded, insulted, and rejected by nonbelievers. No one wants to be treated this way, but this is the reality for Ambassadors who are unafraid to obey God's plan for their lives. Jesus paid the ultimate price for obeying God's plan, Ambassadors should be willing pay the same. We must be willing to lose our temporal lives in order to gain eternal life with God. We will be given eternal rewards for doing this.

Matthew 5:11-12 (NIV)

[11] "Blessed are you when people insult you, persecute you and falsely say all kinds of evil against you because of me.

[12] "Rejoice and be glad, because great is your reward in heaven, for in the same way they persecuted the prophets who were before you."

DISCUSSION QUESTIONS

1. Are heavenly rewards earned or are they a gift?
2. When are heavenly rewards paid?
3. Why should we get rewards for loving our enemies?
4. Will public acts of righteous for receiving rewards from men be rewarded by God?
5. Will Ambassadors receive a reward for enduring persecution?

✞ GOD'S PLAN FOR EVANGELISM AND DISCIPLESHIP ✞

HUMBLENESS

humble

adjective
1.
not proud or arrogant; modest: *to be humble although successful.*

Ambassadors should have humble attitudes and seek ways to serve others, which attracts people to us.

Jesus, although he is Lord, did not come to be served, but to serve others. In this world, the persons of higher position use that authority to get people of lower position to serve them; however, in God's kingdom Ambassadors must be humble and be willing to serve others no matter their position in life.

Mark 10:42-45 (NIV)

[42] Jesus called them together and said, "You know that those who are regarded as rulers of the Gentiles lord it over them, and their high officials exercise authority over them. [43] Not so with you. Instead, whoever wants to become great among you must be your servant, [44] and whoever wants to be first must be slave of all. [45] For even the Son of Man did not come to be served, but to serve, and to give his life as a ransom for many."

Because the Ambassadors believed that Jesus was the Messiah and that they were his closest disciples, they believed that they had high ranks in his kingdom. They began to argue about who among the twelve had the highest rank under Jesus. Jesus told his Ambassadors not to argue over who was the greatest in his kingdom. He told them that the greatest or first in his kingdom must be the very last, and be the servant of all. Ambassadors should not see their positions as greater than others, they should look for ways to serve others at home, at work, or at play. The ones who serve the most will be the highest in Jesus' kingdom.

Mark 9:33-35 (NIV)

[33] They came to Capernaum. When he was in the house, he asked them, "What were you arguing about on the road?" [34] But they kept quiet because on the way they had argued about who was the greatest.

[35] Sitting down, Jesus called the Twelve and said, "Anyone who wants to be first must be the very last, and the servant of all."

Ambassadors should not be afraid to associate with people who are perceived to have low reputations such as sinners and tax collectors, but to be humble and associate with them even if it causes damage to their reputation. Jesus associated with sinners without regard to his reputation because he knew that to reach the lost with his message of salvation that he had to associate with them.

Jesus, by having dinner at Matthew's house and eating with his "sinner" friends, showed by example that we should associate with sinners because they are the ones we are sent to save. Jesus said, "It is not the healthy who need a doctor, but the sick." Jesus also said, "I desire mercy, not sacrifice. For I have not come to call the righteous, but sinners." In other words, Jesus wants Ambassadors who show mercy more than those who religiously appear to follow the law. Remember, no one is able to keep the law in real life, so trying to appear to follow the law for appearance sake is not what Jesus wants. He wants Ambassadors who understand and practice mercy.

Matthew 9:9-13 (NIV)

9 As Jesus went on from there, he saw a man named Matthew sitting at the tax collector's booth. "Follow me," he told him, and Matthew got up and followed him.

10 While Jesus was having dinner at Matthew's house, many tax collectors and sinners came and ate with him and his disciples. 11 When the Pharisees saw this, they asked his disciples, "Why does your teacher eat with tax collectors and sinners?"

12 On hearing this, Jesus said, "It is not the healthy who need a doctor, but the sick. 13 But go and learn what this means: 'I desire mercy, not sacrifice.'[a] For I have not come to call the righteous, but sinners."

Jesus, although he knew that he was the Messiah and worthy of worship, showed his Ambassadors by the example of washing their feet that they should be willing to serve others even by taking up the role of the lowest of servants to meet the needs of others.

John 13:3-17 (NIV)

3 Jesus knew that the Father had put all things under his power, and that he had come from God and was returning to God; 4 so he got up from the meal, took off his outer clothing, and wrapped a towel around his waist. 5 After that, he poured water into a basin and began to wash his disciples' feet, drying them with the towel that was wrapped around him.

6 He came to Simon Peter, who said to him, "Lord, are you going to wash my feet?"

7 Jesus replied, "You do not realize now what I am doing, but later you will understand."

GOD'S PLAN FOR EVANGELISM AND DISCIPLESHIP

[8] "No," said Peter, "you shall never wash my feet."

Jesus answered, "Unless I wash you, you have no part with me."

[9] "Then, Lord," Simon Peter replied, "not just my feet but my hands and my head as well!"

[10] Jesus answered, "Those who have had a bath need only to wash their feet; their whole body is clean. And you are clean, though not every one of you." [11] For he knew who was going to betray him, and that was why he said not everyone was clean.

[12] When he had finished washing their feet, he put on his clothes and returned to his place. "Do you understand what I have done for you?" he asked them. [13] "You call me 'Teacher' and 'Lord,' and rightly so, for that is what I am. [14] Now that I, your Lord and Teacher, have washed your feet, you also should wash one another's feet. [15] I have set you an example that you should do as I have done for you. [16] Very truly I tell you, no servant is greater than his master, nor is a messenger greater than the one who sent him. [17] Now that you know these things, you will be blessed if you do them.

Jesus taught his Ambassadors by using contrasts: pride versus humbleness. An Ambassador should be humble as opposed to proud and self-righteous. Ambassadors are not perfect people, we are sinners saved only by grace. If not for grace we would be destined for eternal punishment because we still miss the mark. Self-righteous people who believe they are saved because of their works are going to be humbled on judgment day. Ambassadors who are humble will be exalted on judgment day.

Luke 18:9-14 (NIV)

⁹ To some who were confident of their own righteousness and looked down on everyone else, Jesus told this parable: ¹⁰ "Two men went up to the temple to pray, one a Pharisee and the other a tax collector. ¹¹ The Pharisee stood by himself and prayed: 'God, I thank you that I am not like other people—robbers, evildoers, adulterers—or even like this tax collector. ¹² I fast twice a week and give a tenth of all I get.'

¹³ "But the tax collector stood at a distance. He would not even look up to heaven, but beat his breast and said, 'God, have mercy on me, a sinner.'

¹⁴ "I tell you that this man, rather than the other, went home justified before God. For all those who exalt themselves will be humbled, and those who humble themselves will be exalted."

The bottom line is Ambassadors should serve others with humble and not arrogant attitudes. We need to attract people and not repel people so that they will be willing to hear and consider our message of salvation.

✞ GOD'S PLAN FOR EVANGELISM AND DISCIPLESHIP ✞

DISCUSSION QUESTIONS

1. What attitude should Ambassadors have to attract unbelievers to themselves?
2. What did Jesus tell the Twelve about who is the greatest in his kingdom?
3. Why should Ambassadors associate with sinners?
4. What did Jesus do to show the Twelve that they should be willing to serve others?
5. Why should an Ambassador be humble as opposed to proud and self-righteousness?

COMPASSION

com·pas·sion

1.
a feeling of deep sympathy and sorrow for another who is stricken by misfortune, accompanied by a strong desire to alleviate the suffering.

mer·cy

1.
compassionate or kindly forbearance shown toward an offender, an enemy, or other person in one's power; compassion, pity, or benevolence: *Have mercy on the poor sinner.*
2.
the discretionary power of a judge to pardon someone or to mitigate punishment, especially to send to prison rather than invoke the death penalty.
3.
an act of kindness, compassion, or favor: *She has performed countless small mercies for her friends and neighbors.*
4.
something that gives evidence of divine favor; blessing: *It was just a mercy we had our seat belts on when it happened.*

pit·y

1.
sympathetic or kindly sorrow evoked by the suffering, distress, or misfortune of another, often leading one to give relief or aid or to show mercy: *to feel pity for a starving child.*
2.
a cause or reason for pity, sorrow, or regret: *What a pity you could not go!*
verb (used with object)

✝ GOD'S PLAN FOR EVANGELISM AND DISCIPLESHIP ✝

3.
to feel pity or compassion for; be sorry for; commiserate with.
verb (used without object)
4.
to have compassion; feel pity.
Idioms
5.
have / take pity, to show mercy or compassion.

Jesus does not want an Ambassador's offerings or sacrifices to God when they are given out of ritual or hypocrisy. He wants Ambassadors to demonstrate the fruit of the Holy Spirit: love, joy, peace, etc. Mercy could be added to this list. Even when Jesus' apostles were criticized by the Pharisees for picking and eating heads of grain because they were hungry, Jesus defended his apostles because it was more important that, through mercy and compassion, their immediate need needed to be satisfied than to ritualistically obey the law of God.

Matthew 12:1-8 (NIV)

[1] At that time Jesus went through the grain fields on the Sabbath. His disciples were hungry and began to pick some heads of grain and eat them. [2] When the Pharisees saw this, they said to him, "Look! Your disciples are doing what is unlawful on the Sabbath."

[3] He answered, "Haven't you read what David did when he and his companions were hungry? [4] He entered the house of God, and he and his companions ate the consecrated bread—which was not lawful for them to do, but only for the priests. [5] Or haven't you read in the Law that the priests on Sabbath duty in the temple desecrate the Sabbath and yet are innocent? [6] I tell you that something greater than the temple is here. [7] If you had known what these words mean, 'I desire mercy, not

sacrifice,'[a] you would not have condemned the innocent. ⁸ For the Son of Man is Lord of the Sabbath."

Jesus criticized the teachers of the law and the Pharisees for not practicing mercy and compassion, although they were religious about tithing. Now tithing is good, but to practice it hypocritically is bad when you pass up immediate opportunities to practice mercy and compassion.

Matthew 23:23 (NIV)

²³ "Woe to you, teachers of the law and Pharisees, you hypocrites! You give a tenth of your spices—mint, dill and cumin. But you have neglected the more important matters of the law—justice, mercy and faithfulness. You should have practiced the latter, without neglecting the former.

There are many instances in the bible where a person in need asked Jesus to have mercy on them and he stopped what he was doing and met their need, and many times with a miracle. The important part is that Jesus immediately met their need. He did not deny or delay their request. He gave them what he had and God did the miraculous. Sometimes Ambassadors have other means to help resolve the problem such as money, time, and other resources. All our resources come from God and we are merely stewards of his resources. We have freely received and we should freely give. As we give, God will refill our supply. Sometimes this sharing of mercy leads to salvation and new followers of God.

Matthew 20:29-34 (NIV)

²⁹ As Jesus and his disciples were leaving Jericho, a large crowd followed him. ³⁰ Two blind men were sitting by the roadside, and when they heard that Jesus was going by, they shouted, "Lord, Son of David, have mercy on us!"

✞ GOD'S PLAN FOR EVANGELISM AND DISCIPLESHIP ✞

³¹ The crowd rebuked them and told them to be quiet, but they shouted all the louder, "Lord, Son of David, have mercy on us!"

³² Jesus stopped and called them. "What do you want me to do for you?" he asked.

³³ "Lord," they answered, "we want our sight."

³⁴ Jesus had compassion on them and touched their eyes. Immediately, they received their sight and followed him.

The key to mercy, compassion, and pity is it starts with an attitude and leads to an action, which sometimes results in salvation and faith in God. God wants his Ambassadors to not only have Christian habits but to live lives full of random acts of kindness.

DISCUSSION QUESTIONS

1. What does Jesus want instead of hypocritical adherence to Jewish rules and regulation?
2. When did Jesus show compassion upon those who asked for it?
3. How should Ambassadors show compassion upon those who ask for it?

GOD'S PLAN FOR EVANGELISM AND DISCIPLESHIP

LOVE

Ambassadors are to obey God's plan, and when they do it shows their love for God; the Father and the Son will love them and Jesus will show himself to them. It all starts with obedience to God and his plan. We can know God through accepting Jesus as our Savoir and we can get to know him better by obeying him as Lord.

John 14:21 (NIV)

21 "Whoever has my commands and keeps them is the one who loves me. The one who loves me will be loved by my Father, and I too will love them and show myself to them."

Those who are not Ambassadors do not know or love God, and it shows because they do not obey God or his plan. Jesus said that in the last days there will be an increase in sin, which is disobedience to God. Most people will become lovers of themselves and obey the cravings of their flesh, and will neglect the needs and wants of others. In other words their love for others will grow cold.

Matthew 24:12 (NIV)

12 Because of the increase of wickedness, the love of most will grow cold.

Love is so important to the well-being of our world that Jesus said that it is the greatest and most important commandment of the Law. We should love God in our vertical relationship with him and we should love our neighbors in our horizontal relationships with them.

✟ GOD'S PLAN FOR EVANGELISM AND DISCIPLESHIP ✟

Mark 12:28-31 (NIV)

²⁸ One of the teachers of the law came and heard them debating. Noticing that Jesus had given them a good answer, he asked him, "Of all the commandments, which is the most important?"

²⁹ "The most important one," answered Jesus, "is this: 'Hear, O Israel: The Lord our God, the Lord is one.'[a] ³⁰ Love the Lord your God with all your heart and with all your soul and with all your mind and with all your strength.'[b] ³¹ The second is this: 'Love your neighbor as yourself.'[c] There is no commandment greater than these."

Love for God and others is important for our world because it takes into account our vertical relationship with God and our horizontal relationships with others. Vertically, God is our creator and has given us every good thing that this world has to offer; and we should love, obey, and worship him for that. Horizontally, when there are more Ambassadors there are more people expressing God's kind of love with others. The world cannot express this kind of unconditional love because it is not within them. A person needs to have God living within them in order to express God's kind of love with others.

The Golden Rule says we should do to others what we would have them do to us. This is a horizontal and proactive kind of love. Most religions teach a kind of love which says don't do to others what you don't want done to you. It is more challenging to be proactive in looking for ways to do good to others than trying to keep from doing bad things to others.

Matthew 7:12 (NIV)

¹² So in everything, do to others what you would have them do to you, for this sums up the Law and the Prophets.

There are many ways to express this horizontal kind of love. Many days present us with impromptu opportunities we can use to help someone in need. On other days we can purposefully plan opportunities to do some good. Either way, God commands us to love our neighbor as our self and Jesus said that when we help others we are helping him. The following verse gives us some ideas for helping others.

Matthew 25:31-40 (NIV)

^{31} "When the Son of Man comes in his glory, and all the angels with him, he will sit on his glorious throne. ^{32} All the nations will be gathered before him, and he will separate the people one from another as a shepherd separates the sheep from the goats. ^{33} He will put the sheep on his right and the goats on his left.

^{34} "Then the King will say to those on his right, 'Come, you who are blessed by my Father; take your inheritance, the kingdom prepared for you since the creation of the world. ^{35} For I was hungry and you gave me something to eat, I was thirsty and you gave me something to drink, I was a stranger and you invited me in, ^{36} I needed clothes and you clothed me, I was sick and you looked after me, I was in prison and you came to visit me.'

^{37} "Then the righteous will answer him, 'Lord, when did we see you hungry and feed you, or thirsty and give you something to drink? ^{38} When did we see you a stranger and invite you in, or needing clothes and clothe you? ^{39} When did we see you sick or in prison and go to visit you?'

^{40} "The King will reply, 'Truly I tell you, whatever you did for one of the least of these brothers and sisters of mine, you did for me.'"

✠ GOD'S PLAN FOR EVANGELISM AND DISCIPLESHIP ✠

We are to love our enemies, too. This is not the kind of love where you have affection toward the person loved. This is the unconditional love that God shares with everyone every day.

Matthew 5:43-45 (NIV)

43 "You have heard that it was said, 'Love your neighbor[a] and hate your enemy.' 44 But I tell you, love your enemies and pray for those who persecute you, 45 that you may be children of your Father in heaven. He causes his sun to rise on the evil and the good, and sends rain on the righteous and the unrighteous."

If our enemy does something bad to us we are not to retaliate and take justice into our own hands to get revenge. God will heal us, replenish what was lost, and repay our enemy.

Luke 6:29-30 (NIV)

29 If someone slaps you on one cheek, turn to them the other also. If someone takes your coat, do not withhold your shirt from them. 30 Give to everyone who asks you, and if anyone takes what belongs to you, do not demand it back.

We are to do good to our enemies, and by forgiving them of doing bad things to us we will be rewarded in heaven. The bottom line for Ambassadors is that we are to represent God and be loving and merciful to our enemies because that is the way that God would have us be.

Luke 6:35-36 (NIV)

35 But love your enemies, do good to them, and lend to them without expecting to get anything back. Then your reward will be great, and you will be children of the Most High, because he is kind to the ungrateful and wicked. 36 Be merciful, just as your Father is merciful.

DISCUSSION QUESTIONS

1. How does an Ambassador show his love for God?
2. Why will the love of most people grow cold?
3. What did Jesus say was the most important commandment?
4. What are some ways to obey the Golden Rule?
5. Why should Ambassadors love their enemies to be like representatives of God?

GOD'S PLAN FOR EVANGELISM AND DISCIPLESHIP

FORGIVENESS

for·give

1.
to grant pardon for or remission of (an offense, debt, etc.); absolve.
2.
to give up all claim on account of; remit (a debt, obligation, etc.).
3.
to grant pardon to (a person).
4.
to cease to feel resentment against: *to forgive one's enemies.*
5.
to cancel an indebtedness or liability of: *to forgive the interest owed on a loan.*

rec·on·cile

1.
to win over to friendliness; cause to become amicable: *to reconcile hostile persons.*
2.
to compose or settle (a quarrel, dispute, etc.).

God wants forgiveness and reconciliation between us and him and between us and others. Man has a sin nature which causes him to sin against God and man. All sins are recorded in the sinner's personal book of life. God has taken the first step to bring about remission of sin, i.e. forgiveness and reconciliation between us and him. He sent his Son into the world to die and pay the penalty for our sins. When we repent of our sins we receive God's gift of forgiveness and are reconciled to him. When we are forgiven by God all of our sins in our personal book are removed. As for forgiveness and reconciliation between us and our fellow man there is an identical principle.

Jesus has already died to pay the penalty for sin. For the sinner to receive forgiveness he must repent of his sin(s) and when the victim forgives them reconciliation can occur.

When an Ambassador is the victim of sin, then when the sinner repents he should forgive the sinner. If the Ambassador will not forgive the sinner then God changes his mind on the forgiveness he has given to the Ambassador and his imputed righteousness is removed and he becomes guilty of all of the sins recorded in his personal book. God wants his Ambassadors to not only know and understand forgiveness, he wants us to practice it. We are God's representatives, and God wants his representatives to practice forgiveness the same way he does.

Matthew 18:23-29 (NIV)

[23] "Therefore, the kingdom of heaven is like a king who wanted to settle accounts with his servants. [24] As he began the settlement, a man who owed him ten thousand bags of gold[a] was brought to him. [25] Since he was not able to pay, the master ordered that he and his wife and his children and all that he had be sold to repay the debt.

[26] "At this the servant fell on his knees before him. 'Be patient with me,' he begged, 'and I will pay back everything.' [27] The servant's master took pity on him, canceled the debt and let him go.

[28] "But when that servant went out, he found one of his fellow servants who owed him a hundred silver coins.[b] He grabbed him and began to choke him. 'Pay back what you owe me!' he demanded.

[29] "His fellow servant fell to his knees and begged him, 'Be patient with me, and I will pay it back.'

[30] "But he refused. Instead, he went off and had the man thrown into prison until he could pay the debt. [31] When the other

servants saw what had happened, they were outraged and went and told their master everything that had happened.

[32] "Then the master called the servant in. 'You wicked servant,' he said, 'I canceled all that debt of yours because you begged me to. [33] Shouldn't you have had mercy on your fellow servant just as I had on you?' [34] In anger his master handed him over to the jailers to be tortured, until he should pay back all he owed.

[35] "This is how my heavenly Father will treat each of you unless you forgive your brother or sister from your heart."

Matthew 6:14-15 (NIV)

[14] For if you forgive other people when they sin against you, your heavenly Father will also forgive you. [15] But if you do not forgive others their sins, your Father will not forgive your sins.

Zacchaeus, a tax collector, is a great example of repentance and forgiveness. Zacchaeus had become rich by cheating people out of their tax money. When he put his faith in Jesus he repented by saying to Jesus that he would give half of his possessions to the poor and by saying he would pay back to those he had stolen from four times the amount of money he had stolen. By faith in God, Zacchaeus received the free gift of forgiveness that Jesus offers through his death on the cross. Jesus forgave him, thus removing all the sins that were written his personal record book, and reconciled him into fellowship with God as a son of Abraham. As for forgiveness between Zacchaeus and those whom he cheated he not only repented, he paid restitution, penalty and interest, which is a good way to show repentance and be restored to those he had cheated.

✠ GOD'S PLAN FOR EVANGELISM AND DISCIPLESHIP ✠

Luke 19:1-10 (NIV)

¹ Jesus entered Jericho and was passing through. ² A man was there by the name of Zacchaeus; he was a chief tax collector and was wealthy. ³ He wanted to see who Jesus was, but because he was short he could not see over the crowd. ⁴ So he ran ahead and climbed a sycamore-fig tree to see him, since Jesus was coming that way.

⁵ When Jesus reached the spot, he looked up and said to him, "Zacchaeus, come down immediately. I must stay at your house today." ⁶ So he came down at once and welcomed him gladly.

⁷ All the people saw this and began to mutter, "He has gone to be the guest of a sinner."

⁸ But Zacchaeus stood up and said to the Lord, "Look, Lord! Here and now I give half of my possessions to the poor, and if I have cheated anybody out of anything, I will pay back four times the amount."

⁹ Jesus said to him, "Today salvation has come to this house, because this man, too, is a son of Abraham. ¹⁰ For the Son of Man came to seek and to save the lost."

In the parable of the prodigal son, Jesus taught two responses to sin and repentance. The prodigal sinned by squandering his inheritance on sinful living. He repented by being willing to be treated as a hired hand and not as a son. His father's response was to forgive him and accept him as a son and celebrate his return with love and a party. The older brother of the prodigal had a different response; he refused to forgive the prodigal. Because he did not forgive his brother he did not experience the love and joy that his father did. And as we learned earlier, when the older brother refused to forgive the prodigal God repented of his forgiveness of the older brother.

One might ask how many times he must I forgive his brother. Peter asked Jesus this question and Jesus said seventy-seven times. Meaning that there is not any set number of times that they should forgive but that they should always be willing to forgive a brother when he is truly repentant.

Matthew 18:21-22 (NIV)

[21] Then Peter came to Jesus and asked, "Lord, how many times shall I forgive my brother or sister who sins against me? Up to seven times?"

[22] Jesus answered, "I tell you, not seven times, but seventy-seven times.

Everyone sins, including God's Ambassadors; it's how we respond to sin that matters. The natural response is to bring charges or retaliate in kind; however, Ambassadors are to be forgiving when people sin against us. We are not to judge hypocritically as if we never sin, because that same type and amount of judgment will be applied to us in the same measure. And, if we are forgiving then that same amount of forgiveness will be applied to us.

We do not have to judge and bring charges for every small and insignificant sin. We have received God's grace of forgiveness, which is undeserved favor, and he wants his Ambassadors to share that grace with others so that others will know him through us. That's not to rule out critical thinking. When the sin is large and significant we should bring charges and we should use biblical truth for making these judgments. There is nothing wrong with critical thinking particularly when it comes to discerning biblical truth. Hypocritical thinking causes dissension while critical thinking brings enlightenment.

Within church discipline, if an Ambassador sins against another Ambassador there is a certain protocol to be followed.

First, the victim is to bring charges to the person who sinned, in private. If he repents then forgiveness can occur. If that sinner does not repent, then the victim is to bring one or two others witnesses, and if the sinner still does not repent then the victim should bring the situation to the church. And if he does not repent then he should be treated as an outsider or an ex-Ambassador.

Luke 6:37-38 (NIV)

^{37} "Do not judge, and you will not be judged. Do not condemn, and you will not be condemned. Forgive, and you will be forgiven. ^{38} Give, and it will be given to you. A good measure, pressed down, shaken together and running over, will be poured into your lap. For with the measure you use, it will be measured to you."

Matthew 7:3-5 (NIV)

^{3} "Why do you look at the speck of sawdust in your brother's eye and pay no attention to the plank in your own eye? ^{4} How can you say to your brother, 'Let me take the speck out of your eye,' when all the time there is a plank in your own eye? ^{5} You hypocrite, first take the plank out of your own eye, and then you will see clearly to remove the speck from your brother's eye."

Matthew 18:15-17 (NIV)

^{15} "If your brother or sister[a] sins,[b] go and point out their fault, just between the two of you. If they listen to you, you have won them over. ^{16} But if they will not listen, take one or two others along, so that 'every matter may be established by the testimony of two or three witnesses.'[c] ^{17} If they still refuse to listen, tell it to the church; and if they refuse to listen even to the church, treat them as you would a pagan or a tax collector."

When an Ambassador remembers that he has sinned against someone, he should go right away to that person and repent and make amends with that person, particularly if that person has pressed charges in court. God does not want his Ambassadors to have unconfessed sin in their lives because it causes problems with their relationship with God and with man.

Matthew 5:23-24 (NIV)

23 "Therefore, if you are offering your gift at the altar and there remember that your brother or sister has something against you, 24 leave your gift there in front of the altar. First go and be reconciled to them; then come and offer your gift.

25 "Settle matters quickly with your adversary who is taking you to court. Do it while you are still together on the way, or your adversary may hand you over to the judge, and the judge may hand you over to the officer, and you may be thrown into prison. 26 Truly, I tell you, you will not get out until you have paid the last penny."

✟ GOD'S PLAN FOR EVANGELISM AND DISCIPLESHIP ✟

DISCUSSION QUESTIONS

1. What has God done to bring about forgiveness and reconciliation between us and him?
2. What does God expect his Ambassadors to do in regard to sin as God's representative?
3. What did Zacchaeus do to receive forgiveness of his sins?
4. What did the prodigal son do that shows his repentance?
5. What is the natural response to when someone sins against us?
6. What is the proper response to when someone sins against us?
7. What is the protocol for when an Ambassador sins against another Ambassador?
8. When an Ambassador remembers that he has sinned against someone, what should he do?

MONEY

Jesus showed his Ambassadors how God works miracles to provide for large immediate financial needs.

When faced with a financial need which is larger than our on hand resources Jesus wants us, through faith, to use what we have and trust him to provide the rest. Jesus performed a miracle when he multiplied the financial resources to meet the said large immediate need. The end result was that God generously met that need and provided more financial resources than what was originally on hand.

Matthew 14:15-18 (NIV)

[15] As evening approached, the disciples came to him and said, "This is a remote place, and it's already getting late. Send the crowds away, so they can go to the villages and buy themselves some food."

[16] Jesus replied, "They do not need to go away. You give them something to eat."

[17] "We have here only five loaves of bread and two fish," they answered.

[18] "Bring them here to me," he said.

When we have been trying to meet our financial needs on our own strength and have no fruit to show for our labor we should ask for God's help and try again. We should trust God and through faith he will make our efforts fruitful.

☦ GOD'S PLAN FOR EVANGELISM AND DISCIPLESHIP ☦

John 21:3-7 (NIV)

³ "I'm going out to fish," Simon Peter told them, and they said, "We'll go with you." So they went out and got into the boat, but that night they caught nothing.

⁴ Early in the morning, Jesus stood on the shore, but the disciples did not realize that it was Jesus.

⁵ He called out to them, "Friends, haven't you any fish?"

"No," they answered.

⁶ He said, "Throw your net on the right side of the boat and you will find some." When they did, they were unable to haul the net in because of the large number of fish.

⁷ Then the disciple whom Jesus loved said to Peter, "It is the Lord!" As soon as Simon Peter heard him say, "It is the Lord," he wrapped his outer garment around him (for he had taken it off) and jumped into the water.

When God provides he does not provide low quality resources, he provides the same or better quality resources than what is needed.

John 2:1-11 (NIV)

¹ On the third day a wedding took place at Cana in Galilee. Jesus' mother was there, ² and Jesus and his disciples had also been invited to the wedding. ³ When the wine was gone, Jesus' mother said to him, "They have no more wine."

⁴ "Woman,[a] why do you involve me?" Jesus replied. "My hour has not yet come."

⁵ His mother said to the servants, "Do whatever he tells you."

⁶ Nearby stood six stone water jars, the kind used by the Jews for ceremonial washing, each holding from twenty to thirty gallons.[b]

⁷ Jesus said to the servants, "Fill the jars with water"; so they filled them to the brim.

⁸ Then he told them, "Now draw some out and take it to the master of the banquet."

They did so, ⁹ and the master of the banquet tasted the water that had been turned into wine. He did not realize where it had come from, though the servants who had drawn the water knew. Then he called the bridegroom aside ¹⁰ and said, "Everyone brings out the choice wine first and then the cheaper wine after the guests have had too much to drink; but you have saved the best till now."

¹¹ What Jesus did here in Cana of Galilee was the first of the signs through which he revealed his glory; and his disciples believed in him.

Ambassadors are sons of God and thus are exempt from taxation, however Jesus wants us to pay our taxes in order to not offend the government. God will help us find the financial resources to pay the taxes, using a miracle if necessary.

Matthew 17:24-27 (NIV)

²⁴ After Jesus and his disciples arrived in Capernaum, the collectors of the two-drachma temple tax came to Peter and asked, "Doesn't your teacher pay the temple tax?"

²⁵ "Yes, he does," he replied.

When Peter came into the house, Jesus was the first to speak. "What do you think, Simon?" he asked. "From whom do the kings of the earth collect duty and taxes—from their own children or from others?"

²⁶ "From others," Peter answered.

"Then the children are exempt," Jesus said to him. ²⁷ "But so that we may not cause offense, go to the lake and throw out your line. Take the first fish you catch; open its mouth and you will find a four-drachma coin. Take it and give it to them for my tax and yours."

DISCUSSION QUESTIONS

1. When an Ambassador has been unfruitful in their efforts or do not have enough financial resources to meet an immediate need what should they do?
2. When God provides financial resources what quality or quantity of resources does he provide?

✝ GOD'S PLAN FOR EVANGELISM AND DISCIPLESHIP ✝

GUIDANCE

guidance

the act or function of guiding; leadership; direction.

guide

to supply (a person) with advice or counsel, as in practical or spiritual affair

Jesus said that he would send the Holy Spirit to guide Ambassadors into all truth that would help them with their situations. Today we can ask the Father to help us with our particular needs that achieve God's plan.

John 16:13 (NIV)

[13] But when he, the Spirit of truth, comes, he will guide you into all the truth. He will not speak on his own; he will speak only what he hears, and he will tell you what is yet to come.

The Holy Spirit will guide us into decisions that we could not make without God's help. For example, Joseph was considering other ways to deal with Mary's pregnancy, but God gave him another way which was to marry her and to raise the baby as his own. Ambassadors should always seek God's guidance in making important decisions.

Matthew 1:18-21 (NIV)

[18] This is how the birth of Jesus the Messiah came about[a]: His mother Mary was pledged to be married to Joseph, but before they came together, she was found to be pregnant through the Holy Spirit. [19] Because Joseph her husband was faithful to the law, and yet[b] did not want to expose her to public disgrace, he had in mind to divorce her quietly.

²⁰ But after he had considered this, an angel of the Lord appeared to him in a dream and said, "Joseph son of David, do not be afraid to take Mary home as your wife, because what is conceived in her is from the Holy Spirit. ²¹ She will give birth to a son, and you are to give him the name Jesus,[c] because he will save his people from their sins."

Ambassadors should be open to change their plans if God guides them into another way.

For example, the wise men were told not to return to Herod after visiting baby Jesus, so they traveled home by another route. And Joseph was told by God to travel to Egypt to keep Jesus safe because Herod was planning on killing him.

Matthew 2:12-15 (NIV)

¹² And having been warned in a dream not to go back to Herod, they returned to their country by another route.

¹³ When they had gone, an angel of the Lord appeared to Joseph in a dream. "Get up," he said, "take the child and his mother and escape to Egypt. Stay there until I tell you, for Herod is going to search for the child to kill him."

¹⁴ So he got up, took the child and his mother during the night and left for Egypt, ¹⁵ where he stayed until the death of Herod. And so was fulfilled what the Lord had said through the prophet: "Out of Egypt I called my son."

DISCUSSION QUESTIONS

1. What kind of guidance does the Holy Spirit give?
2. Why should Ambassadors seek God's guidance when they already have their own plan to follow?

✝ GOD'S PLAN FOR EVANGELISM AND DISCIPLESHIP ✝

PROTECTION

pro·tect

to defend or guard from attack, invasion, loss, annoyance, insult, etc.; cover or shield from injury or danger.

God protects his Ambassadors from temporal and eternal harm. Satan must get permission from God in order to attack Ambassadors temporally; but he cannot harm them eternally at all.

John 17:11-15 (NIV)

[11] I will remain in the world no longer, but they are still in the world, and I am coming to you. Holy Father, protect them by the power of[a] your name, the name you gave me, so that they may be one as we are one. [12] While I was with them, I protected them and kept them safe by[b] that name you gave me. None has been lost except the one doomed to destruction so that Scripture would be fulfilled.

[13] "I am coming to you now, but I say these things while I am still in the world, so that they may have the full measure of my joy within them. [14] I have given them your word and the world has hated them, for they are not of the world any more than I am of the world. [15] My prayer is not that you take them out of the world but that you protect them from the evil one

When the storms of life affect Ambassadors and unbelievers there are different outcomes. For Ambassadors, they withstand the difficulty and do not crash and fall because they are under God's protection for following God's plan. But for unbelievers, they crash and fall because they are not under God's protection because they do not follow God's plan. So Ambassadors have protection that unbelievers do not have. Satan cannot harm our souls or take away our eternal life with God." The temporal environment is Satan's domain and he can cause us temporal harm, but cannot cause us eternal harm. As long as we follow Jesus he will protect us eternally toward our eternal home in heaven

Matthew 7:24-27 (NIV)

24 "Therefore everyone who hears these words of mine and puts them into practice is like a wise man who built his house on the rock. 25 The rain came down, the streams rose, and the winds blew and beat against that house; yet it did not fall, because it had its foundation on the rock. 26 But everyone who hears these words of mine and does not put them into practice is like a foolish man who built his house on sand. 27 The rain came down, the streams rose, and the winds blew and beat against that house, and it fell with a great crash."

Speaking of storms, the disciples found themselves in a physical storm that caused great waves to wash over their boat and threaten their very lives. Jesus was with them in the boat sleeping. They were so afraid that they went to Jesus to save them and woke him up. He criticized the disciples for having little faith because they did not handle the problem themselves. Jesus rebuked the waves and the water became calm. Jesus expected the disciples to rebuke the waves just as he did. They had the authority to do so, but they were so afraid that that they forgot to use it. Today when we find ourselves facing physical or spiritual danger we should remember to fear not and to trust God to give us wisdom and strength to resolve the problem with God's help. If we have been trusting God and following God's plan for our lives we can expect a good outcome

Matthew 8:23-27 (NIV)

23 Then he got into the boat and his disciples followed him. 24 Suddenly a furious storm came up on the lake, so that the waves swept over the boat. But Jesus was sleeping. 25 The

disciples went and woke him, saying, "Lord, save us! We're going to drown!"

²⁶ He replied, "You of little faith, why are you so afraid?" Then he got up and rebuked the winds and the waves, and it was completely calm.

²⁷ The men were amazed and asked, "What kind of man is this? Even the winds and the waves obey him!"

Jesus is our protector, he protects Ambassadors from bad circumstances and bad people. Jesus provides eternal protection by providing eternal life. No one else can provide eternal life and protection but Jesus. Satan comes to steal, kill, and destroy. We need protection from Satan.

John 10:7-15 (NIV)

⁷ Therefore Jesus said again, "Very truly I tell you, I am the gate for the sheep. ⁸ All who have come before me are thieves and robbers, but the sheep have not listened to them. ⁹ I am the gate; whoever enters through me will be saved.[a] They will come in and go out, and find pasture. ¹⁰ The thief comes only to steal and kill and destroy; I have come that they may have life, and have it to the full.

¹¹ "I am the good shepherd. The good shepherd lays down his life for the sheep. ¹² The hired hand is not the shepherd and does not own the sheep. So when he sees the wolf coming, he abandons the sheep and runs away. Then the wolf attacks the flock and scatters it. ¹³ The man runs away because he is a hired hand and cares nothing for the sheep.

¹⁴ "I am the good shepherd; I know my sheep and my sheep know me— ¹⁵ just as the Father knows me and I know the Father—and I lay down my life for the sheep.

✟ GOD'S PLAN FOR EVANGELISM AND DISCIPLESHIP ✟

DISCUSSION QUESTIONS

1. Who does Jesus want to protect to his Ambassadors from?
2. Why does God protect Ambassadors during the storms of life?
3. Why does not God protect unbelievers during the storms of life?
4. What does Satan come to do to the Ambassador?

SICKNESS

Jesus healed people with all kinds of ailments: leprosy, demon-possession, paralysis, bleeding, blindness, muteness, deafness, fever, a shriveled hand, and others. The key factor in each of the healings was faith. Ambassadors should have faith and remember who they are when they try to help heal a person. They are representatives of God with the authority to perform miracles in Jesus' name as God works through them.

Mark 9:14-29 (NIV)

[14] When they came to the other disciples, they saw a large crowd around them and the teachers of the law arguing with them. [15] As soon as all the people saw Jesus, they were overwhelmed with wonder and ran to greet him.

[16] "What are you arguing with them about?" he asked.

[17] A man in the crowd answered, "Teacher, I brought you my son, who is possessed by a spirit that has robbed him of speech. [18] Whenever it seizes him, it throws him to the ground. He foams at the mouth, gnashes his teeth and becomes rigid. I asked your disciples to drive out the spirit, but they could not."

[19] "You unbelieving generation," Jesus replied, "how long shall I stay with you? How long shall I put up with you? Bring the boy to me."

[20] So they brought him. When the spirit saw Jesus, it immediately threw the boy into a convulsion. He fell to the ground and rolled around, foaming at the mouth.

[21] Jesus asked the boy's father, "How long has he been like this?"

☦ GOD'S PLAN FOR EVANGELISM AND DISCIPLESHIP ☦

"From childhood," he answered. ²² "It has often thrown him into fire or water to kill him. But if you can do anything, take pity on us and help us."

²³ "'If you can'?" said Jesus. "Everything is possible for one who believes."

²⁴ Immediately the boy's father exclaimed, "I do believe; help me overcome my unbelief!"

²⁵ When Jesus saw that a crowd was running to the scene, he rebuked the impure spirit. "You deaf and mute spirit," he said, "I command you, come out of him and never enter him again."

²⁶ The spirit shrieked, convulsed him violently and came out. The boy looked so much like a corpse that many said, "He's dead." ²⁷ But Jesus took him by the hand and lifted him to his feet, and he stood up.

²⁸ After Jesus had gone indoors, his disciples asked him privately, "Why couldn't we drive it out?"

²⁹ He replied, "This kind can come out only by prayer."[a]

Mark 10:46-52 (NIV)

⁴⁶ Then they came to Jericho. As Jesus and his disciples, together with a large crowd, were leaving the city, a blind man, Bartimaeus (which means "son of Timaeus"), was sitting by the roadside begging. ⁴⁷ When he heard that it was Jesus of Nazareth, he began to shout, "Jesus, Son of David, have mercy on me!"

⁴⁸ Many rebuked him and told him to be quiet, but he shouted all the more, "Son of David, have mercy on me!"

⁴⁹ Jesus stopped and said, "Call him."

So they called to the blind man, "Cheer up! On your feet! He's calling you." ⁵⁰ Throwing his cloak aside, he jumped to his feet and came to Jesus.

⁵¹ "What do you want me to do for you?" Jesus asked him.

The blind man said, "Rabbi, I want to see."

⁵² "Go," said Jesus, "your faith has healed you." Immediately he received his sight and followed Jesus along the road.

There were times when Jesus said that the person being healed had "great faith." For example when a centurion came to him asking him to heal his servant, Jesus wanted to go to the centurion's home to heal the servant, but the centurion said Jesus did not have to go to his house, all Jesus had to do was just say the word and the servant would be healed; that's great faith in Jesus's authority to heal.

Matthew 8:5-10 (NIV)

⁵ When Jesus had entered Capernaum, a centurion came to him, asking for help. ⁶ "Lord," he said, "my servant lies at home paralyzed, suffering terribly."

⁷ Jesus said to him, "Shall I come and heal him?"

⁸ The centurion replied, "Lord, I do not deserve to have you come under my roof. But just say the word, and my servant will be healed. ⁹ For I myself am a man under authority, with soldiers under me. I tell this one, 'Go,' and he goes; and that one, 'Come,' and he comes. I say to my servant, 'Do this,' and he does it."

¹⁰ When Jesus heard this, he was amazed and said to those following him, "Truly I tell you, I have not found anyone in Israel with such great faith.

Another example is the time when a gentile Canaanite woman came to Jesus and asked for healing for her daughter who had suffered terribly from demon-possession. Jesus did not heal her right away; he stated that Jews were worthy of God's healing because they were God's children; not gentiles. However the woman persisted saying that even "dogs," another name for gentiles, were allowed to be healed as if they were getting "seconds" that had fallen from the master's table. Jesus admired her great faith and healed her daughter that very hour.

Matthew 15:21-28 (NIV)

[21] Leaving that place, Jesus withdrew to the region of Tyre and Sidon. [22] A Canaanite woman from that vicinity came to him, crying out, "Lord, Son of David, have mercy on me! My daughter is demon-possessed and suffering terribly."

[23] Jesus did not answer a word. So his disciples came to him and urged him, "Send her away, for she keeps crying out after us."

[24] He answered, "I was sent only to the lost sheep of Israel."

[25] The woman came and knelt before him. "Lord, help me!" she said.

[26] He replied, "It is not right to take the children's bread and toss it to the dogs."

[27] "Yes it is, Lord," she said. "Even the dogs eat the crumbs that fall from their master's table."

[28] Then Jesus said to her, "Woman, you have great faith! Your request is granted." And her daughter was healed at that moment.

DISCUSSION QUESTIONS

1. What should an Ambassador have in order to be used by God to heal someone?
2. What does Jesus say about those who have "great faith"?
3. What does an Ambassador need in order to work miracles in Jesus' name?

DEATH

Jesus raised people from the dead. He is God and therefore he has the authority to raise people from the dead. He would touch the dead person and that person would get up; or he would speak a command, for example, "Little girl, I say to you, get up!" Another time he said, "Young man, I say to you, get up!"

Mark 5:38-42 (NIV)

38 When they came to the home of the synagogue leader, Jesus saw a commotion, with people crying and wailing loudly. 39 He went in and said to them, "Why all this commotion and wailing? The child is not dead but asleep." 40 But they laughed at him.

After he put them all out, he took the child's father and mother and the disciples who were with him, and went in where the child was. 41 He took her by the hand and said to her, *"Talitha koum!"* (which means "Little girl, I say to you, get up!"). 42 Immediately the girl stood up and began to walk around (she was twelve years old). At this they were completely astonished.

Luke 7:11-14 (NIV)

11 Soon afterward, Jesus went to a town called Nain, and his disciples and a large crowd went along with him. 12 As he approached the town gate, a dead person was being carried out—the only son of his mother, and she was a widow. And a large crowd from the town was with her. 13 When the Lord saw her, his heart went out to her and he said, "Don't cry."

14 Then he went up and touched the bier they were carrying him on, and the bearers stood still. He said, "Young man, I say to you, get up!"

☦ GOD'S PLAN FOR EVANGELISM AND DISCIPLESHIP ☦

The person who came to Jesus on the dead person's behalf speaks words of faith, for example, "My daughter has just died. But come and put your hand on her, and she will live." Or on another occasion Jesus told the dead person's advocate to "Don't be afraid, just believe, and she will be healed."

Matthew 9:18 (NIV)

[18] While he was saying this, a synagogue leader came and knelt before him and said, "My daughter has just died. But come and put your hand on her, and she will live."

Luke 8:49-50 (NIV)

[49] While Jesus was still speaking, someone came from the house of Jairus, the synagogue leader. "Your daughter is dead," he said. "Don't bother the teacher anymore."

[50] Hearing this, Jesus said to Jairus, "Don't be afraid; just believe, and she will be healed."

Ambassadors, as God's representatives, have the authority to wake a person up from the dead, if God wills it to be done.

DISCUSSION QUESTIONS

1. What does an Ambassador need to have and do in order to raise a person from the dead?
2. Besides the Ambassador, who needs to have faith in order to help raise a person from the dead?

✟ GOD'S PLAN FOR EVANGELISM AND DISCIPLESHIP ✟

DISOBEDIANCE

sin

1.

transgression of divine law:

the sin of Adam.

2.

any act regarded as such a transgression, especially a willful or deliberate violation of some religious or moral principle.

obey

1.

to comply with or follow the commands, restrictions, wishes, or instructions of:

to obey one's parents.

2.

to comply with or follow (a command, restriction, wish, instruction, etc.).

3.

to submit or conform in action to (some guiding principle, impulse, one's conscience, etc.).

dis·o·bey

to neglect or refuse to obey.

For non-believers there is a problem, they have sin on their personal record books and they have a sin nature which leads them to commit sins. On judgment day God looks at these personal record books, sees the sins, and pronounces a guilty verdict and sends the non-believer to the lake of fire for all eternity.

✟ GOD'S PLAN FOR EVANGELISM AND DISCIPLESHIP ✟

For Ambassadors there is no problem; they have no sin on their personal record books, and they have a sin nature too, which leads them to commit sins. On judgment day God looks at their personal record books and sees no sins because they have been forgiven. He pronounces an innocent verdict and sends the Ambassador to heaven for all eternity.

During their lives, Ambassadors learn and obey God's plan. They have been saved by repentance and faith in God's word and can see and understand God's plan. Unbelievers have not been saved and they do not obey God's plan because they cannot see nor understand God's plan and have their own plan that they are following.

Jesus said that he who loves him will obey God's plan, will have fellowship with God, and experience eternal life. He said that he who does not love him will not obey God's plan.

John 14:23-24 (NIV)

[23] Jesus replied, "Anyone who loves me will obey my teaching. My Father will love them, and we will come to them and make our home with them. [24] Anyone who does not love me will not obey my teaching. These words you hear are not my own; they belong to the Father who sent me."

Matthew 19:16-17 (NIV)

[16] Just then a man came up to Jesus and asked, "Teacher, what good thing must I do to get eternal life?"

[17] "Why do you ask me about what is good?" Jesus replied. "There is only One who is good. If you want to enter life, keep the commandments."

Jesus said that you cannot claim salvation because your parents are saved, you must make a personal decision on your own to repent of your own plan and commit to obey God's plan with Jesus as Lord of your life, then with God's help you can produce the fruit that God desires.

Matthew 3:8-10 (NIV)

[8] Produce fruit in keeping with repentance. [9] And do not think you can say to yourselves, 'We have Abraham as our father.' I tell you that out of these stones God can raise up children for Abraham. [10] The ax is already at the root of the trees, and every tree that does not produce good fruit will be cut down and thrown into the fire.

Jesus said that our desire to commit sin, such as evil thoughts, sexual immorality, etc., comes from our sin nature which is within our heart. This sin nature tempts us to sin and without faith in God's word and the Holy Spirit which strengthens us, we disobey God and sin.

Mark 7:14-23 (NIV)

[14] Again Jesus called the crowd to him and said, "Listen to me, everyone, and understand this. [15] Nothing outside a person can defile them by going into them. Rather, it is what comes out of a person that defiles them." [16] [a]

[17] After he had left the crowd and entered the house, his disciples asked him about this parable. [18] "Are you so dull?" he asked. "Don't you see that nothing that enters a person from the outside can defile them? [19] For it doesn't go into their heart but into their stomach, and then out of the body." (In saying this, Jesus declared all foods clean.)

[20] He went on: "What comes out of a person is what defiles them. [21] For it is from within, out of a person's heart, that evil thoughts come—sexual immorality, theft, murder, [22] adultery, greed, malice, deceit, lewdness, envy, slander, arrogance and folly. [23] All these evils come from inside and defile a person."

DISCUSSION QUESTIONS

1. What is the problem for non-believers?
2. Why is there no problem for Ambassadors?
3. How does a person show their love for God?
4. What happens to those who do not produce good fruit?
5. What leads us to sin and become unclean?

✟ GOD'S PLAN FOR EVANGELISM AND DISCIPLESHIP ✟

JUDGEMENT

There will be two judgments; one for Ambassadors and another for unbelievers.

There are certain unbelievers who do not believe in a judgment day or in a place called hell. What a surprise is waiting for them. The bible says that all of the dead unbelievers will hear the voice of Jesus and will be raised to face condemnation by him whether they believe in life after death or not. Some unbelievers believe that life ends when they die here on earth, but that is not true. Ambassadors believe that there will be a judgment day and on that day they will be judged innocent and be sent to heaven.

John 5:25-29 (NIV)

[25] Very truly I tell you, a time is coming and has now come when the dead will hear the voice of the Son of God and those who hear will live. [26] For as the Father has life in himself, so he has granted the Son also to have life in himself. [27] And he has given him authority to judge because he is the Son of Man.

[28] "Do not be amazed at this, for a time is coming when all who are in their graves will hear his voice [29] and come out—those who have done what is good will rise to live, and those who have done what is evil will rise to be condemned.

God allows the good and evil to live together here on earth until judgment day and then he will send his angels to collect both. The good and evil will then be separated from each other. The evil will then be condemned and the good will be found innocent.

✞ GOD'S PLAN FOR EVANGELISM AND DISCIPLESHIP ✞

Matthew 13:24-30 (NIV)

24 Jesus told them another parable: "The kingdom of heaven is like a man who sowed good seed in his field. 25 But while everyone was sleeping, his enemy came and sowed weeds among the wheat, and went away. 26 When the wheat sprouted and formed heads, then the weeds also appeared.

27 "The owner's servants came to him and said, 'Sir, didn't you sow good seed in your field? Where then did the weeds come from?'

28 "'An enemy did this,' he replied.

"The servants asked him, 'Do you want us to go and pull them up?'

29 "'No,' he answered, 'because while you are pulling the weeds, you may uproot the wheat with them. 30 Let both grow together until the harvest. At that time I will tell the harvesters: First collect the weeds and tie them in bundles to be burned; then gather the wheat and bring it into my barn.'"

How bad will hell be? How is it described in the bible? It is described as a lake of fire, an unquenchable fire, a place where the worm does not die, a fiery furnace where there will be weeping and gnashing of teeth. It is really bad because it was created for the devil and his demons. Heaven is really good because it was created for God and his angels. Jesus did not describe heaven as much as he did hell, but we can know certain things that are inferred by contrast with hell. In hell there is Satan and demons, all the worst evil doers of all time, sickness, and despair. In heaven there is God in all three persons, angels, perfection, and hope.

Mark 9:43-48 (NIV)

[43] If your hand causes you to stumble, cut it off. It is better for you to enter life maimed than with two hands to go into hell, where the fire never goes out. [44] [a] [45] And if your foot causes you to stumble, cut it off. It is better for you to enter life crippled than to have two feet and be thrown into hell. [46] [b] [47] And if your eye causes you to stumble, pluck it out. It is better for you to enter the kingdom of God with one eye than to have two eyes and be thrown into hell, [48] where

"'the worms that eat them do not die,
and the fire is not quenched.'"[c]

Matthew 13:36-46 (NIV)

[36] Then he left the crowd and went into the house. His disciples came to him and said, "Explain to us the parable of the weeds in the field."

[37] He answered, "The one who sowed the good seed is the Son of Man. [38] The field is the world, and the good seed stands for the people of the kingdom. The weeds are the people of the evil one, [39] and the enemy who sows them is the devil. The harvest is the end of the age, and the harvesters are angels.

[40] "As the weeds are pulled up and burned in the fire, so it will be at the end of the age. [41] The Son of Man will send out his angels, and they will weed out of his kingdom everything that causes sin and all who do evil. [42] They will throw them into the blazing furnace, where there will be weeping and gnashing of teeth. [43] Then the righteous will shine like the sun in the kingdom of their Father. Whoever has ears, let them hear.

[44] "The kingdom of heaven is like treasure hidden in a field. When a man found it, he hid it again, and then in his joy went and sold all he had and bought that field.

⁴⁵ "Again, the kingdom of heaven is like a merchant looking for fine pearls. ⁴⁶ When he found one of great value, he went away and sold everything he had and bought it."

Good fruit are tangible deeds that a person does in obedience to God which affect other people's lives for the better. Anyone who does not produce good fruit will be thrown into the lake of fire. Ambassadors who obey God's plan will produce good fruit. Unbelievers do not obey God's plan and will not produce good fruit and will be condemned to the lake of fire.

Matthew 3:8-10 (NIV)

⁸ Produce fruit in keeping with repentance. ⁹ And do not think you can say to yourselves, 'We have Abraham as our father.' I tell you that out of these stones God can raise up children for Abraham. ¹⁰ The ax is already at the root of the trees, and every tree that does not produce good fruit will be cut down and thrown into the fire.

John 15:4-6 (NIV)

⁴ Remain in me, as I also remain in you. No branch can bear fruit by itself; it must remain in the vine. Neither can you bear fruit unless you remain in me.

⁵ "I am the vine; you are the branches. If you remain in me and I in you, you will bear much fruit; apart from me you can do nothing. ⁶ If you do not remain in me, you are like a branch that is thrown away and withers; such branches are picked up, thrown into the fire and burned."

Because of the aforementioned, everyone has an incentive to follow God's plan. The question is where do you want to spend eternity? The answer is simple: heaven. Remember salvation is by grace through faith in Jesus as our Savior. Rewards are earned by following God's plan through the power of the Holy Spirit with Jesus as our Lord.

✞ GOD'S PLAN FOR EVANGELISM AND DISCIPLESHIP ✞

DISCUSSION QUESTIONS

1. How should unbelievers feel about judgement day?
2. How should Ambassadors feel about judgement day?
3. What should a person do once he has discovered eternal life?
4. What happens to the kind of branch that bears good fruit and what happens to the kind of branch that does not bear good fruit?

WORKS

Unbelievers have a sin problem and that problem keeps them from receiving eternal life. They think they can resolve this problem by doing good works. They hope they can do enough good works to outweigh their sins and earn a place in heaven. God's judgment does not work that way. God looks at your personal record book and if he sees even one sin he will judge you guilty and send you to hell for all eternity, no matter how many good works are recorded. Your own righteousness by way of not doing bad works and of doing good works will not get you into heaven.

Luke 18:9-14 (NIV)

[9] To some who were confident of their own righteousness and looked down on everyone else, Jesus told this parable: [10] "Two men went up to the temple to pray, one a Pharisee and the other a tax collector. [11] The Pharisee stood by himself and prayed: 'God, I thank you that I am not like other people—robbers, evildoers, adulterers—or even like this tax collector. [12] I fast twice a week and give a tenth of all I get.'

[13] "But the tax collector stood at a distance. He would not even look up to heaven, but beat his breast and said, 'God, have mercy on me, a sinner.'

[14] "I tell you that this man, rather than the other, went home justified before God. For all those who exalt themselves will be humbled, and those who humble themselves will be exalted."

Some non-believers will be surprised when they come before God on judgement day and find out that their good works did not save them from going to hell. They did not have a relationship with Jesus, did not accept him as Savior, and did not obey him as Lord.

✞ GOD'S PLAN FOR EVANGELISM AND DISCIPLESHIP ✞

Matthew 7:21-23 (NIV)

²¹ "Not everyone who says to me, 'Lord, Lord,' will enter the kingdom of heaven, but only the one who does the will of my Father who is in heaven. ²² Many will say to me on that day, 'Lord, Lord, did we not prophesy in your name and in your name drive out demons and in your name perform many miracles?' ²³ Then I will tell them plainly, 'I never knew you. Away from me, you evildoers!'

Jesus called some Pharisees and teachers of the law hypocrites because they placed their man made traditions and rules equal to God's word. God says that obeying these traditions and rules is doing good works in vain because they cannot be used to offset their sins. God wants us to put our faith in him and to obey his plan, not man's plan.

Mark 7:1-8 (NIV)

¹ The Pharisees and some of the teachers of the law who had come from Jerusalem gathered around Jesus ² and saw some of his disciples eating food with hands that were defiled, that is, unwashed. ³ (The Pharisees and all the Jews do not eat unless they give their hands a ceremonial washing, holding to the tradition of the elders. ⁴ When they come from the marketplace they do not eat unless they wash. And they observe many other traditions, such as the washing of cups, pitchers and kettles.[a])

⁵ So the Pharisees and teachers of the law asked Jesus, "Why don't your disciples live according to the tradition of the elders instead of eating their food with defiled hands?"

⁶ He replied, "Isaiah was right when he prophesied about you hypocrites; as it is written:

"'These people honor me with their lips,
but their hearts are far from me.
⁷ They worship me in vain;
their teachings are merely human rules.'[b]

⁸ You have let go of the commands of God and are holding on to human traditions."

Some non-believers want to know what good works they must do to get eternal life and Jesus' says that they have to obey the commandments. But because of man's sinful nature it is natural for man to sin, get sins recorded in their personal record books, and thus be disqualified from obtaining eternal life.

Matthew 19:16-17 (NIV)

¹⁶ Just then a man came up to Jesus and asked, "Teacher, what good thing must I do to get eternal life?"

¹⁷ "Why do you ask me about what is good?" Jesus replied. "There is only One who is good. If you want to enter life, keep the commandments."

Some non-believers may ask, "What is the point of doing good works if they will not get you eternal life." Jesus said that first you must be saved and then your good works will be rewarded in heaven. Good works, in obedience to God's plan, are rewarded but do not get you eternal life. Eternal life is by grace through faith in Jesus Christ as your Savior.

✟ GOD'S PLAN FOR EVANGELISM AND DISCIPLESHIP ✟

Matthew 23:25-26 (NIV)

²⁵ "Woe to you, teachers of the law and Pharisees, you hypocrites! You clean the outside of the cup and dish, but inside they are full of greed and self-indulgence. ²⁶ Blind Pharisee! First clean the inside of the cup and dish, and then the outside also will be clean.

So non-believers may ask "What good work can a person do to resolve the sin problem?" and "What good works does God require? The answer is: to do the work that God requires is to believe in Jesus Christ as your Savior.

John 6:28-29 (NIV)

⁸ Then they asked him, "What must we do to do the works God requires?"

²⁹ Jesus answered, "The work of God is this: to believe in the one he has sent."

DISCUSSION QUESTIONS

1. What good are good works if they do not get you into heaven?
2. Under what condition does good works get rewarded in heaven?
3. What did Jesus say about doing good works that get you into heaven?

✞ GOD'S PLAN FOR EVANGELISM AND DISCIPLESHIP ✞

ETERNAL LIFE

Eternal life is by grace through faith, not works. Eternal life is a gift because Jesus has done all the work and offers it to us as a free gift when we place our faith in him as our Savior.

Eternal life is where you spend eternity with God in heaven if you have put your faith in Jesus Christ. Eternal punishment is where you spend your eternity with Satan in hell if you refuse to put your faith in Jesus.

John 3:16 (NIV)

[16] For God so loved the world that he gave his one and only Son, that whoever believes in him shall not perish but have eternal life.

John 17:3 (NIV)

[3] Now this is eternal life: that they know you, the only true God, and Jesus Christ, whom you have sent.

John 5:24 (NIV)

[24] "Very truly I tell you, whoever hears my word and believes him who sent me has eternal life and will not be judged but has crossed over from death to life."

Jesus is the Savior of the entire world and the Samaritans learned this from listening to the testimony of the Samaritan woman whom he met at the well and then again from listening to his message first hand.

☥ GOD'S PLAN FOR EVANGELISM AND DISCIPLESHIP ☥

John 4:39-42 (NIV)

³⁹ Many of the Samaritans from that town believed in him because of the woman's testimony, "He told me everything I ever did." ⁴⁰ So when the Samaritans came to him, they urged him to stay with them, and he stayed two days. ⁴¹ And because of his words many more became believers.

⁴² They said to the woman, "We no longer believe just because of what you said; now we have heard for ourselves, and we know that this man really is the Savior of the world."

To experience eternal life four things must occur: one must be redeemed, be forgiven, be born again, and be baptized in the Holy Spirit. These all occur at once when you place your faith in Jesus. Redemption and forgiveness frees people from judgment and going to hell for all eternity. Being born again creates a new spirit and makes it possible to receive the Holy Spirit. The baptism of the Holy Spirit empowers Ambassador to work God's plan with power.

First, let's talk about redemption. The remedy for our sin nature is redemption. We all are born with a sin nature which leads us to commit sins. Our sin nature is the root cause of our problem for committing sins, so much that the bible says that we are slaves to sin. Redemption occurs because Jesus died on the cross in our place. His death paid the ransom to purchase us out of judgment and eternal punishment in hell.

John 8:34 (NIV)

³⁴ Jesus replied, "Very truly I tell you, everyone who sins is a slave to sin."

John 8:35-36 (NIV)

[35] Now a slave has no permanent place in the family, but a son belongs to it forever. [36] So if the Son sets you free, you will be free indeed.

Mark 10:43-45 (NIV)

[43] "Not so with you. Instead, whoever wants to become great among you must be your servant, [44] and whoever wants to be first must be slave of all. [45] For even the Son of Man did not come to be served, but to serve, and to give his life as a ransom for many."

Second, let's talk about forgiveness. The remedy for our sins being recorded in our personal books in heaven is forgiveness. Forgiveness occurs because of Jesus' death on the cross. All of our sins are taken from our books and laid on Jesus. He died to pay the price for our sins so that they would be forgiven. For those who put their faith in him their personal record is cleared of all sins.

Third, let's talk about being born again. To be born again is to be regenerated with a new spirit. Being born again makes it possible for Ambassadors to enter the kingdom of God, to have their spiritual eyes opened so that they can satisfy their spiritual thirst and hunger by reading the word of God, and make it possible to experience a relationship with God.

John 3:3-5 (NIV)

[3] Jesus replied, "Very truly I tell you, no one can see the kingdom of God unless they are born again.[a]"

⁴ "How can someone be born when they are old?" Nicodemus asked. "Surely they cannot enter a second time into their mother's womb to be born!"

⁵ Jesus answered, "Very truly I tell you, no one can enter the kingdom of God unless they are born of water and the Spirit."

John 1:12-13 (NIV)

¹² Yet to all who did receive him, to those who believed in his name, he gave the right to become children of God— ¹³ children born not of natural descent, nor of human decision or a husband's will, but born of God.

Fourth and finally, let's talk about being baptized with the Holy Spirit. Jesus is the one who baptizes with the Holy Spirit; John the Baptist said so and so did Jesus. And Jesus said that the baptism with the Holy Spirit would give them the power needed to work God's plan effectively.

Luke 3:16 (NIV)

¹⁶ John answered them all, "I baptize you with[a] water. But one who is more powerful than I will come, the straps of whose sandals I am not worthy to untie. He will baptize you with[b] the Holy Spirit and fire."

Luke 24:49 (NIV)

⁴⁹ "I am going to send you what my Father has promised; but stay in the city until you have been clothed with power from on high."

That's right, the Holy Spirit would work through the Ambassadors to give them the correct words to say when presenting the gospel message, receiving revelation as to future events, guidance, teaching, remembrance, etc.

Mark 13:11 (NIV)

[11] Whenever you are arrested and brought to trial, do not worry beforehand about what to say. Just say whatever is given you at the time, for it is not you speaking, but the Holy Spirit.

Luke 2:26-27 (NIV)

[26] It had been revealed to him by the Holy Spirit that he would not die before he had seen the Lord's Messiah. [27] Moved by the Spirit, he went into the temple courts. When the parents brought in the child Jesus to do for him what the custom of the Law required.

John 14:26 (NIV)

[26] But the Advocate, the Holy Spirit, whom the Father will send in my name, will teach you all things and will remind you of everything I have said to you.

✣ GOD'S PLAN FOR EVANGELISM AND DISCIPLESHIP ✣

DISCUSSION QUESTIONS

1. Why is eternal life by grace through faith?
2. What four things must occur before a person experiences eternal life?
3. Why does the bible say that "everyone who sins is a slave to sin?"

INCARNATION

Incarnation

1.

an incarnate being or form.

2.

a living being embodying a deity or spirit.

3.

assumption of human form or nature.

4.

the Incarnation, (*sometimes lowercase*) *Theology.* the doctrine that the second person of the Trinity assumed human form in the person of Jesus Christ and is completely both God and man.

Before Jesus created heaven and earth he pre-existed as a spirit. In fact, Jesus is eternal, he has no beginning or end. He knew, before the creation of the world, that man would fall into sin and be in need of salvation from God's judgment. He knew that man would need a savior to accomplish this salvation. He knew that the savoir would have to be sinless; otherwise, there would need to be a savoir for the savior. Only God is sinless and so he would have to be the savior. Salvation was a part of God's plan before the creation of the world. So, at the right time the incarnation took place, i.e. God assumed human form.

John 1:1-3 (NIV)

[1] In the beginning was the Word, and the Word was with God, and the Word was God. [2] He was with God in the beginning. [3] Through him all things were made; without him nothing was made that has been made.

✟ GOD'S PLAN FOR EVANGELISM AND DISCIPLESHIP ✟

John 1:14 (NIV)

14 The Word became flesh and made his dwelling among us. We have seen his glory, the glory of the one and only Son, who came from the Father, full of grace and truth.

God chose a virgin named Mary and a carpenter named Joseph to be the mother and stepfather for the child Jesus. Joseph was the stepfather because God was Jesus' father. When the angel told Mary that she was going to be a mother she asked him how this was going to happen since she was a virgin. The angel told her how the Holy Spirit was going to overshadow her so that the child Jesus would be called the Son of God. Jesus is uniquely the Son of God. Jesus is both fully human and fully God. Because God is his father, Jesus was born without a sin nature.

Matthew 1:18-20 (NIV)

18 This is how the birth of Jesus the Messiah came about[a]: His mother Mary was pledged to be married to Joseph, but before they came together, she was found to be pregnant through the Holy Spirit. 19 Because Joseph her husband was faithful to the law, and yet[b] did not want to expose her to public disgrace, he had in mind to divorce her quietly.

20 But after he had considered this, an angel of the Lord appeared to him in a dream and said, "Joseph, son of David, do not be afraid to take Mary home as your wife, because what is conceived in her is from the Holy Spirit.

Luke 1:31-34 (NIV)

31 You will conceive and give birth to a son, and you are to call him Jesus. 32 He will be great and will be called the Son of the Most High. The Lord God will give him the throne of his father

David, ³³ and he will reign over Jacob's descendants forever; his kingdom will never end."

³⁴ "How will this be," Mary asked the angel, "since I am a virgin?"

Our savior is called Jesus and Immanuel because of what the names mean in relation to God being born of a women in the form of a baby boy: the incarnation. Jesus means "the Lord saves" and Immanuel means "God with us." He lived up to his name Jesus by obeying God's plan, which included him saving us from our sins by dying on the cross. And He is called "God with us" because he is God in human form living amongst us on earth.

Matthew 1:21-23 (NIV)

²¹ She will give birth to a son, and you are to give him the name Jesus,[a] because he will save his people from their sins."

²² All this took place to fulfill what the Lord had said through the prophet: ²³ "The virgin will conceive and give birth to a son, and they will call him Immanuel"[b] (which means "God with us").

God directly said that Jesus was his son when Jesus was being baptized. He spoke and said, to Jesus "You are my Son."

Mark 1:9-11 (NIV)

⁹ At that time Jesus came from Nazareth in Galilee and was baptized by John in the Jordan. ¹⁰ Just as Jesus was coming up out of the water, he saw heaven being torn open and the Spirit descending on him like a dove. ¹¹ And a voice came from heaven: "You are my Son, whom I love; with you I am well pleased."

Jesus, when asked by the high priest if he was the Christ, he answered with a simple, "I am," meaning yes.

Mark 14:61-62 (NIV)

⁶¹ But Jesus remained silent and gave no answer.

Again the high priest asked him, "Are you the Messiah, the Son of the Blessed One?"

⁶² "I am," said Jesus. "And you will see the Son of Man sitting at the right hand of the Mighty One and coming on the clouds of heaven."

Jesus is the Messiah because through his virgin birth he proved that he was God incarnate. Being God incarnate means that Jesus was born sinless, he had no sin nature. All through the Old Testament the sacrifice for sin had to be spotless. And Jesus' personal record was spotless because he was born God, and he lived a sinless life. Ambassadors need to believe in the virgin birth because no other religion has a founder and leader who was born this way. This makes Christianity unique.

DISCUSSION QUESTIONS

1. Why was it important that Jesus be born without a sin nature?
2. What about the incarnation makes Christianity different from all other faiths?

✟ GOD'S PLAN FOR EVANGELISM AND DISCIPLESHIP ✟

MIRACLES

Jesus's miracles proved that he was the Messiah. The Jews, disciples, and demons all had firsthand experiences with Jesus performing miracles.

The Jews who had seen Jesus perform many miracles did not believe he was the Christ even though he had plainly said that he was the Christ. The Jews, understanding that Jesus had claimed to be God, wanted to stone him because they believed that what he had said was blasphemous.

John 10:22-33 (NIV)

22 Then came the Festival of Dedication[a] at Jerusalem. It was winter, 23 and Jesus was in the temple courts walking in Solomon's Colonnade. 24 The Jews who were there gathered around him, saying, "How long will you keep us in suspense? If you are the Messiah, tell us plainly."

25 Jesus answered, "I did tell you, but you do not believe. The works I do in my Father's name testify about me, 26 but you do not believe because you are not my sheep. 27 My sheep listen to my voice; I know them, and they follow me. 28 I give them eternal life, and they shall never perish; no one will snatch them out of my hand. 29 My Father, who has given them to me, is greater than all[b]; no one can snatch them out of my Father's hand. 30 I and the Father are one."

31 Again his Jewish opponents picked up stones to stone him, 32 but Jesus said to them, "I have shown you many good works from the Father. For which of these do you stone me?"

33 "We are not stoning you for any good work," they replied, "but for blasphemy, because you, a mere man, claim to be God."

Jesus demonstrated to the Jews that he was the Christ through the miraculous healing and the forgiving the sins of the paralytic. Once again the Jews wanted to stone him for blasphemy because he forgave someone's sins, something which only God can do.

Mark 2:1-12 (NIV)

¹ A few days later, when Jesus again entered Capernaum, the people heard that he had come home. ² They gathered in such large numbers that there was no room left, not even outside the door, and he preached the word to them. ³ Some men came, bringing to him a paralyzed man, carried by four of them. ⁴ Since they could not get him to Jesus because of the crowd, they made an opening in the roof above Jesus by digging through it and then lowered the mat the man was lying on. ⁵ When Jesus saw their faith, he said to the paralyzed man, "Son, your sins are forgiven."

⁶ Now some teachers of the law were sitting there, thinking to themselves, ⁷ "Why does this fellow talk like that? He's blaspheming! Who can forgive sins but God alone?"

⁸ Immediately Jesus knew in his spirit that this was what they were thinking in their hearts, and he said to them, "Why are you thinking these things? ⁹ Which is easier: to say to this paralyzed man, 'Your sins are forgiven,' or to say, 'Get up, take your mat and walk'? ¹⁰ But I want you to know that the Son of Man has authority on earth to forgive sins." So he said to the man, ¹¹ "I tell you, get up, take your mat and go home." ¹² He got up, took his mat and walked out in full view of them all. This amazed everyone and they praised God, saying, "We have never seen anything like this!"

The disciples witnessed the miracle of Jesus walking on the water and leading Peter to do the same. After seeing this the disciples in the boat worshipped him and saying, "Truly you are the Son of God."

Matthew 14:25-33 (NIV)

[25] Shortly before dawn Jesus went out to them, walking on the lake. [26] When the disciples saw him walking on the lake, they were terrified. "It's a ghost," they said, and cried out in fear.

[27] But Jesus immediately said to them: "Take courage! It is I. Don't be afraid."

[28] "Lord, if it's you," Peter replied, "tell me to come to you on the water."

[29] "Come," he said.

Then Peter got down out of the boat, walked on the water and came toward Jesus. [30] But when he saw the wind, he was afraid and, beginning to sink, cried out, "Lord, save me!"

[31] Immediately Jesus reached out his hand and caught him. "You of little faith," he said, "why did you doubt?"

[32] And when they climbed into the boat, the wind died down. [33] Then those who were in the boat worshiped him, saying, "Truly you are the Son of God."

Demons are no friends of Christ and do not worship him, either, but they know who he is, the Son of God and because of Jesus' authority over them they have to obey him. Jesus performed miracles of rebuking and casting out demons.

Luke 4:33-36 (NIV)

[33] In the synagogue there was a man possessed by a demon, an impure spirit. He cried out at the top of his voice, [34] "Go away!

✝ GOD'S PLAN FOR EVANGELISM AND DISCIPLESHIP ✝

What do you want with us, Jesus of Nazareth? Have you come to destroy us? I know who you are—the Holy One of God!"

[35] "Be quiet!" Jesus said sternly. "Come out of him!" Then the demon threw the man down before them all and came out without injuring him.

[36] All the people were amazed and said to each other, "What words these are! With authority and power he gives orders to impure spirits and they come out!"

Luke 4:41 (NIV)

[41] Moreover, demons came out of many people, shouting, "You are the Son of God!" But he rebuked them and would not allow them to speak, because they knew he was the Messiah.

Mark 3:11 (NIV)

[11] Whenever the impure spirits saw him, they fell down before him and cried out, "You are the Son of God."

Ambassadors need to understand that it is important to know and obey God's plan so that God will work miraculously through them to accomplish his will. Miracles still happen today because God is the same God who worked them in biblical times. God wants to reveal himself and he will through miracles.

DISCUSSION QUESTIONS

1. Why did the Jews not believe that Jesus was God even after witnessing the miracles?
2. Why should Ambassadors believe that God performs miracles today?
3. Why do Ambassadors have authority over demons?

✟ GOD'S PLAN FOR EVANGELISM AND DISCIPLESHIP ✟

ATONEMENT

Jesus made atonement for our sins when he shed his blood and died on a cross while being crucified for our sins. His atonement for sin made it possible for people to become forgiven and reconciled to God.

Jesus death on the cross was always a central part of God's plan from the beginning of time and was prophesized by prophets in the Old Testament. Jesus explained this to the Twelve but they did not understand because the meaning of his death was hidden from them.

Luke 18:31-34 (NIV)

[31] Jesus took the Twelve aside and told them, "We are going up to Jerusalem, and everything that is written by the prophets about the Son of Man will be fulfilled. [32] He will be delivered over to the Gentiles. They will mock him, insult him and spit on him; [33] they will flog him and kill him. On the third day he will rise again."

[34] The disciples did not understand any of this. Its meaning was hidden from them, and they did not know what he was talking about.

Jesus spoke of the purpose of the atonement in his teaching about communion. He said that communion, involving his body and blood, demonstrated the new covenant between God and man. The old covenant involved animal sacrifices with the spilling of blood of a spotless lamb. The new covenant involved the sacrifice and shedding of blood of the sinless Lamb of God: Jesus Christ. The atonement under the new covenant is made effective by repentance from sin and faith in Jesus Christ as the Messiah.

✞ GOD'S PLAN FOR EVANGELISM AND DISCIPLESHIP ✞

Matthew 26:26-29 (NIV)

²⁶ While they were eating, Jesus took bread, and when he had given thanks, he broke it and gave it to his disciples, saying, "Take and eat; this is my body."

²⁷ Then he took a cup, and when he had given thanks, he gave it to them, saying, "Drink from it, all of you. ²⁸ This is my blood of the[b] covenant, which is poured out for many for the forgiveness of sins. ²⁹ I tell you, I will not drink from this fruit of the vine from now on until that day when I drink it new with you in my Father's kingdom."

Under the old covenant within the temple, there were three areas: the courts, the Holy Place and the Most Holy Place. There was a curtain separating the Holy Place from the Most Holy Place. The Most Holy Place was the place where the high priest entered only once per year to atone for the sins of the people. On the day that Jesus was crucified, when he cried out, "It is finished" that curtain was torn in two from top to bottom, the earth shook and the rocks split. The centurion, who was standing there near Jesus heard Jesus' last words and saw him give up his spirit said, "Surely this man was the Son of God. Jesus' statement "It is finished" means to be paid in full, signifying the end of the need of the old covenant sacrifices.

Mark 15:37-39 (NIV)

³⁷ With a loud cry, Jesus breathed his last.

³⁸ The curtain of the temple was torn in two from top to bottom. ³⁹ And when the centurion, who stood there in front of Jesus, saw how he died,[a] he said, "Surely this man was the Son of God!"

John 19:30 (NIV)

30 When he had received the drink, Jesus said, "It is finished." With that, he bowed his head and gave up his spirit.

Before his arrest, Jesus explained to the disciples that he was going to be betrayed to the chief priests and teachers of the law who would condemn him to death and hand him over to the Gentiles. The Gentles would mock him, spit on him, flog him and kill him; and three days later he would rise from the dead. The disciples after hearing Jesus explain this were filled with grief and despair because they had hoped that Jesus was going to be a conquering king who would free them from Roman rule. So when Jesus told them that he was going to die and be resurrected they did not understand. They only heard the part about him dying and could not understand that his death and resurrection would bring victory over sin and make his kingdom possible. In almost every verse that Jesus talked about his death, he also spoke of his resurrection. The disciples had never experienced a resurrection before and did not understand it until after Jesus' resurrection; then they understood that his death and resurrection would bring victory and hope.

Matthew 17:22-23 (NIV)

22 When they came together in Galilee, he said to them, "The Son of Man is going to be delivered into the hands of men. 23 They will kill him, and on the third day he will be raised to life." And the disciples were filled with grief.

Mark 10:33-34 (NIV)

33 "We are going up to Jerusalem," he said, "and the Son of Man will be delivered over to the chief priests and the teachers of the law. They will condemn him to death and will hand him over to the Gentiles, 34 who will mock him and spit on him, flog him and kill him. Three days later he will rise."

✞ GOD'S PLAN FOR EVANGELISM AND DISCIPLESHIP ✞

Jesus told his disciples that his death would be like a kernel of wheat that when it falls to the ground and dies it remains only a single seed, but after it is buried it sprouts a blade of wheat producing many more seeds. Ambassadors are the "many more seeds" who die to their selfish sin nature to only to be born again and lead other unbelievers to become Ambassadors and experience eternal life.

John 12:23-25 (NIV)

[23] Jesus replied, "The hour has come for the Son of Man to be glorified. [24] Very truly I tell you, unless a kernel of wheat falls to the ground and dies, it remains only a single seed. But if it dies, it produces many seeds. [25] Anyone who loves their life will lose it, while anyone who hates their life in this world will keep it for eternal life.

DISCUSSION QUESTIONS

1. What did Jesus' atoning death on the cross accomplish?
2. Why did the disciples not know that Jesus' death and resurrection would bring victory and hope?

✧ GOD'S PLAN FOR EVANGELISM AND DISCIPLESHIP ✧

RESURRECTION

After Jesus' death the disciples were scared and scattered. They had yet to understand that Jesus' death was part of God's plan for victory. They were scared because they thought that since they were Jesus' disciples they were next, and so they scattered.

Matthew 26:31-32 (NIV)

³¹ Then Jesus told them, "This very night you will all fall away on account of me, for it is written:

"'I will strike the shepherd,
and the sheep of the flock will be scattered.'[a]

³² But after I have risen, I will go ahead of you into Galilee."

The story of the resurrection begins with the empty tomb. The chief priests and the Pharisees remembered that Jesus had predicted his resurrection and so they went to Pilate and asked him to have the tomb protected from the disciples so that they could not make it appear that the resurrection had happened by stealing the body and claim that it was missing because of the resurrection,.

Matthew 27:62-66 (NIV)

⁶² The next day, the one after Preparation Day, the chief priests and the Pharisees went to Pilate. ⁶³ "Sir," they said, "we remember that while he was still alive that deceiver said, 'After three days I will rise again.' ⁶⁴ So give the order for the tomb to be made secure until the third day. Otherwise, his disciples may come and steal the body and tell the people that he has been raised from the dead. This last deception will be worse than the first."

⁶⁵ "Take a guard," Pilate answered. "Go, make the tomb as secure as you know how." ⁶⁶ So they went and made the tomb secure by putting a seal on the stone and posting the guard.

Three days after Jesus' death an angel appeared to the guard and rolled away the stone. The guard after seeing all of this fainted and later ran away. Mary Magdalene and the other Mary went to look at the tomb and met the angel and he told them that Jesus was no longer there, and that he had risen. The angel invited them to look into the tomb to verify that what he had told them was true. One of the reasons the resurrection is so believable is because of the many first hand facts and evidence that are stated in the bible.

Matthew 28:1-7 (NIV)

¹ After the Sabbath, at dawn on the first day of the week, Mary Magdalene and the other Mary went to look at the tomb.

² There was a violent earthquake, for an angel of the Lord came down from heaven and, going to the tomb, rolled back the stone and sat on it. ³ His appearance was like lightning, and his clothes were white as snow. ⁴ The guards were so afraid of him that they shook and became like dead men.

⁵ The angel said to the women, "Do not be afraid, for I know that you are looking for Jesus, who was crucified. ⁶ He is not here; he has risen, just as he said. Come and see the place where he lay. ⁷ Then go quickly and tell his disciples: 'He has risen from the dead and is going ahead of you into Galilee. There you will see him.' Now I have told you."

After his resurrection Jesus made appearances to many people. The first appearance was to Mary Magdalene, then to the other women.

Mark 16:9 (NIV)

⁹ When Jesus rose early on the first day of the week, he appeared first to Mary Magdalene, out of whom he had driven seven demons.

Matthew 28:5-10 (NIV)

⁵ The angel said to the women, "Do not be afraid, for I know that you are looking for Jesus, who was crucified. ⁶ He is not here; he has risen, just as he said. Come and see the place where he lay. ⁷ Then go quickly and tell his disciples: 'He has risen from the dead and is going ahead of you into Galilee. There you will see him.' Now I have told you."

⁸ So the women hurried away from the tomb, afraid yet filled with joy, and ran to tell his disciples. ⁹ Suddenly Jesus met them. "Greetings," he said. They came to him, clasped his feet and worshiped him. ¹⁰ Then Jesus said to them, "Do not be afraid. Go and tell my brothers to go to Galilee; there they will see me."

These women went back to the disciples to tell them of Jesus' appearance but when the disciples heard what the women had told them, they did not believe them.

Luke 24:9-11 (NIV)

⁹ When they came back from the tomb, they told all these things to the Eleven and to all the others. ¹⁰ It was Mary Magdalene, Joanna, Mary the mother of James, and the others with them who told this to the apostles. ¹¹ But they did not believe the women, because their words seemed to them like nonsense.

Jesus next appeared to two men, one being a man named Cleopas. The two men reported this to the others, but they did not believe them either.

Mark 16:12-13 (NIV)

[12] Afterward Jesus appeared in a different form to two of them while they were walking in the country. [13] These returned and reported it to the rest; but they did not believe them either.

It was not until Jesus appeared to the disciples, minus Thomas, that they believed that he had been resurrected. He showed them the evidence of his wounds and he ate some fish in their presence to give them evidence that he was not a spirit. Jesus went away. Then a disciple named Thomas came back to the place where the disciples stayed. The disciples told Thomas of Jesus' appearance but he would not believe them unless he saw Jesus with his own eyes. Later Jesus appeared to Thomas and let him touch his wounds and then he believed.

John 20:19-20 (NIV)

[19] On the evening of that first day of the week, when the disciples were together, with the doors locked for fear of the Jewish leaders, Jesus came and stood among them and said, "Peace be with you!" [20] After he said this, he showed them his hands and side. The disciples were overjoyed when they saw the Lord.

John 20:24-29 (NIV)

[24] Now Thomas (also known as Didymus[a]), one of the Twelve, was not with the disciples when Jesus came. [25] So the other disciples told him, "We have seen the Lord!"

But he said to them, "Unless I see the nail marks in his hands and put my finger where the nails were, and put my hand into his side, I will not believe."

[26] A week later his disciples were in the house again, and Thomas was with them. Though the doors were locked, Jesus came and stood among them and said, "Peace be with you!" [27] Then he said to Thomas, "Put your finger here; see my hands. Reach out your hand and put it into my side. Stop doubting and believe."

[28] Thomas said to him, "My Lord and my God!"

[29] Then Jesus told him, "Because you have seen me, you have believed; blessed are those who have not seen and yet have believed."

Ambassadors and unbelievers should believe in the resurrection because of all of the first hand evidence that is presented in the bible. Because of the resurrection we can believe that Jesus is the promised Messiah and believe that his death on the cross can atone for the sins of everyone. Not every person is going to believe in spite of the evidence and Ambassadors should continue to share God's plan to them and others so that they can see and experience God's love through us.

✞ GOD'S PLAN FOR EVANGELISM AND DISCIPLESHIP ✞

DISCUSSION QUESTIONS

1. After Jesus' death, what were the chief priests and the Pharisees afraid of?
2. What caused the guard to faint and then to run away?
3. What are some of the first hand facts and evidence of Jesus' resurrection?
4. What was the disciples' first reaction to hearing about Jesus's resurrection?
5. What was the disciples' reaction to Jesus' resurrection after seeing and touching him?

ASCENSION

Ascension

1.

the act of ascending; ascent.

2.

the Ascension, the bodily ascending of Christ from earth to heaven

Jesus predicted to his disciples that he would leave them and then come back to them. He did this so that when it did happen it would cause his disciples to believe in him even more because it would be another prediction that came true, like his resurrection from the dead.

John 14:27-29 (NIV)

[27] Peace I leave with you; my peace I give you. I do not give to you as the world gives. Do not let your hearts be troubled and do not be afraid.

[28] "You heard me say, 'I am going away and I am coming back to you.' If you loved me, you would be glad that I am going to the Father, for the Father is greater than I. [29] I have told you now before it happens, so that when it does happen you will believe."

Before his ascension into heaven, Jesus told his disciples that he would send the Holy Spirit from heaven to comfort and guide them. Just as Jesus had been with them physically (limited to being in one place at a time) the Holy Spirit would be with them with no limits on how many places he could be at the same time. The Holy Spirit could be anywhere and everywhere at the same time. The Holy Spirit, the Spirit of truth, would guide them into all truth. He would know

✠ GOD'S PLAN FOR EVANGELISM AND DISCIPLESHIP ✠

everything that Jesus knows and would be able to tell them of future things to come.

John 14:15-20 (NIV)

¹⁵ "If you love me, keep my commands. ¹⁶ And I will ask the Father, and he will give you another advocate to help you and be with you forever— ¹⁷ the Spirit of truth. The world cannot accept him, because it neither sees him nor knows him. But you know him, for he lives with you and will be[a] in you. ¹⁸ I will not leave you as orphans; I will come to you. ¹⁹ Before long, the world will not see me anymore, but you will see me. Because I live, you also will live. ²⁰ On that day you will realize that I am in my Father, and you are in me, and I am in you."

John 16:5-16 (NIV)

⁵ "but now I am going to him who sent me. None of you asks me, 'Where are you going?' ⁶ Rather, you are filled with grief because I have said these things. ⁷ But very truly I tell you, it is for your good that I am going away. Unless I go away, the Advocate will not come to you; but if I go, I will send him to you. ⁸ When he comes, he will prove the world to be in the wrong about sin and righteousness and judgment: ⁹ about sin, because people do not believe in me; ¹⁰ about righteousness, because I am going to the Father, where you can see me no longer; ¹¹ and about judgment, because the prince of this world now stands condemned.

¹² "I have much more to say to you, more than you can now bear. ¹³ But when he, the Spirit of truth, comes, he will guide you into all the truth. He will not speak on his own; he will speak only what he hears, and he will tell you what is yet to come. ¹⁴ He will glorify me because it is from me that he will receive what he will make known to you. ¹⁵ All that belongs to the Father is mine. That is why I said the Spirit will receive from me what he will make known to you."

¹⁶ Jesus went on to say, "In a little while you will see me no more, and then after a little while you will see me."

When the time had finally come for his ascension, Jesus led the disciples to a place in the vicinity of Bethany and left them physically and was taken up into heaven. Now the disciples were not filled with grief but were filled with great joy and they were continually at the temple praising God.

Luke 24:50-53 (NIV)

⁵⁰ When he had led them out to the vicinity of Bethany, he lifted up his hands and blessed them. ⁵¹ While he was blessing them, he left them and was taken up into heaven. ⁵² Then they worshiped him and returned to Jerusalem with great joy. ⁵³ And they stayed continually at the temple, praising God.

DISCUSSION QUESTIONS

1. Why did Jesus tell his disciples that he was going to go away and then return?
2. What would the Holy Spirit do after Jesus had ascended?

RETURN

The bible clearly states that Jesus is the Son of God, the Messiah, when talking about his return to earth after his ascension into heaven. The bible describes his return as Jesus siting on his throne coming back on the clouds of the sky, with power and great glory, and with his angels. The event will be visible for all of the inhabitants of earth to see just as lightning that comes from the east is visible even in the west. And unbelievers will mourn because they will realize that they had made the wrong choice, and that it is too late to change their mind.

Matthew 25:31 (NIV)

31 "When the Son of Man comes in his glory, and all the angels with him, he will sit on his glorious throne.

Matthew 24:27 (NIV)

27 For as lightning that comes from the east is visible even in the west, so will be the coming of the Son of Man.

Matthew 24:30 (NIV)

30 "Then will appear the sign of the Son of Man in heaven. And then all the peoples of the earth[a] will mourn when they see the Son of Man coming on the clouds of heaven, with power and great glory.[b]

Immediately before Jesus' return there will be signs in the sky: the sun will become dark, the moon will not give its light, stars will fall from the sky, and the heavenly bodies will be shaken. People will faint from terror, fearing what is coming on the world.

✝ GOD'S PLAN FOR EVANGELISM AND DISCIPLESHIP ✝

Mark 13:24-26 (NIV)

24 "But in those days, following that distress,

"'the sun will be darkened,
and the moon will not give its light;
25 the stars will fall from the sky,
and the heavenly bodies will be shaken.'[a]

26 "At that time people will see the Son of Man coming in clouds with great power and glory."

Luke 21:25-28 (NIV)

25 "There will be signs in the sun, moon and stars. On the earth, nations will be in anguish and perplexity at the roaring and tossing of the sea. 26 People will faint from terror, apprehensive of what is coming on the world, for the heavenly bodies will be shaken. 27 At that time they will see the Son of Man coming in a cloud with power and great glory. 28 When these things begin to take place, stand up and lift up your heads, because your redemption is drawing near."

No one knows the date or time of his return, not even the angels or Jesus, only the Father knows. But when he does return people will be doing normal day activities just like people were doing during Noah's day just before the flood. They will be eating and drinking, marrying and giving in marriage. Also, Ambassadors will be taken mysteriously, called the rapture. It will be like two people, an Ambassador and an unbeliever will be working together and the Ambassador will be taken and the unbeliever will be left behind. Remember, salvation is a free offer, but it is limited time offer. When Jesus returns it will be too late to take him up on that free offer. So you must be ready because Jesus' will return at a time when you do not expect him.

Matthew 24:36-42 (NIV)

36 "But about that day or hour no one knows, not even the angels in heaven, nor the Son,[a] but only the Father. 37 As it was in the days of Noah, so it will be at the coming of the Son of Man. 38 For in the days before the flood, people were eating and drinking, marrying and giving in marriage, up to the day Noah entered the ark; 39 and they knew nothing about what would happen until the flood came and took them all away. That is how it will be at the coming of the Son of Man. 40 Two men will be in the field; one will be taken and the other left. 41 Two women will be grinding with a hand mill; one will be taken and the other left."

42 "Therefore keep watch, because you do not know on what day your Lord will come."

Jesus wants his Ambassadors to be ready when he returns. He wants them to be working God's plan until the day they die or Jesus returns. If the Ambassador figures that Jesus is taking a long time in returning and begins to live like an unbeliever, woe to him. Jesus will assign him a place in hell, instead of heaven. After salvation it is very important that the new Ambassador receive discipleship to learn and obey God's plan for the rest of their lives so that they can live with confidence that eternal life with God is theirs for now and forever.

Luke 12:35-46 (NIV)

35 "Be dressed ready for service and keep your lamps burning, 36 like servants waiting for their master to return from a wedding banquet, so that when he comes and knocks they can immediately open the door for him. 37 It will be good for those servants whose master finds them watching when he comes. Truly I tell you, he will dress himself to serve, will have them recline at the table and will come and wait on them. 38 It will be good for those servants whose master finds them ready, even if

✝ GOD'S PLAN FOR EVANGELISM AND DISCIPLESHIP ✝

he comes in the middle of the night or toward daybreak. ³⁹ But understand this: If the owner of the house had known at what hour the thief was coming, he would not have let his house be broken into. ⁴⁰ You also must be ready, because the Son of Man will come at an hour when you do not expect him."

⁴¹ Peter asked, "Lord, are you telling this parable to us, or to everyone?"

⁴² The Lord answered, "Who then is the faithful and wise manager, whom the master puts in charge of his servants to give them their food allowance at the proper time? ⁴³ It will be good for that servant whom the master finds doing so when he returns. ⁴⁴ Truly I tell you, he will put him in charge of all his possessions. ⁴⁵ But suppose the servant says to himself, 'My master is taking a long time in coming,' and he then begins to beat the other servants, both men and women, and to eat and drink and get drunk. ⁴⁶ The master of that servant will come on a day when he does not expect him and at an hour he is not aware of. He will cut him to pieces and assign him a place with the unbelievers."

DISCUSSION QUESTIONS

1. How would you describe Jesus' return?
2. Who knows the timing of Jesus' return?
3. What will unbelievers be doing when Jesus returns?
4. What will Ambassador be doing when Jesus returns?

✟ GOD'S PLAN FOR EVANGELISM AND DISCIPLESHIP ✟

COMMITMENT

Jesus wants Ambassadors who have counted the cost of being his Ambassador and are still willing to commit to following him.

Following Jesus can cost an Ambassador his freedom, family, all of his material possessions, and even the loss of his life. Jesus causes prospective believers to consider stepping outside of their comfort zones to become an Ambassador for Jesus. Fear of loss may cause a prospective believer to reject Jesus' offer of eternal life. Fear of loss is short sighted because material possessions are temporary; i.e. here today and gone tomorrow, but eternal life is here today and for all eternity.

In times of Christian persecution where Ambassadors are being thrown into jail or executed for their faith in Jesus an Ambassador must be committed to Jesus to the death. If a prospective believer rejects Jesus' offer of eternal life because he does not want to deny himself material gain, freedom, or loss of life, then they are choosing, eternal punishment in hell.

Luke 14:27-35 (NIV)

[27] And whoever does not carry their cross and follow me cannot be my disciple.

[28] "Suppose one of you wants to build a tower. Won't you first sit down and estimate the cost to see if you have enough money to complete it? [29] For if you lay the foundation and are not able to finish it, everyone who sees it will ridicule you, [30] saying, 'This person began to build and wasn't able to finish.'

[31] "Or suppose a king is about to go to war against another king. Won't he first sit down and consider whether he is able with ten thousand men to oppose the one coming against him with twenty thousand? [32] If he is not able, he will send a

delegation while the other is still a long way off and will ask for terms of peace. ³³ In the same way, those of you who do not give up everything you have cannot be my disciples.

³⁴ "Salt is good, but if it loses its saltiness, how can it be made salty again? ³⁵ It is fit neither for the soil nor for the manure pile; it is thrown out.

"Whoever has ears to hear, let them hear."

Mark 8:34-38 (NIV)

³⁴ Then he called the crowd to him along with his disciples and said: "Whoever wants to be my disciple must deny themselves and take up their cross and follow me. ³⁵ For whoever wants to save their life[a] will lose it, but whoever loses their life for me and for the gospel will save it. ³⁶ What good is it for someone to gain the whole world, yet forfeit their soul? ³⁷ Or what can anyone give in exchange for their soul? ³⁸ If anyone is ashamed of me and my words in this adulterous and sinful generation, the Son of Man will be ashamed of them when he comes in his Father's glory with the holy angels."

Jesus said that if an Ambassador denies Jesus then Jesus will deny him at the judgement. On the other hand if he acknowledges Jesus then Jesus will acknowledge them at the judgement.

Matthew 10:32-33 (NIV)

³² "Whoever acknowledges me before others, I will also acknowledge before my Father in heaven. ³³ But whoever disowns me before others, I will disown before my Father in heaven."

Some unbelievers procrastinate in making a decision giving excuses for not accepting Jesus instantly, they do not realize that a non-decision is a decision to go to eternal punishment in hell. They don't realize that although eternal life is a free offer, it is also a limited time offer. It's a limited time offer because it's available only while the unbeliever is alive or until Jesus returns.

Luke 9:57-62 (NIV)

57 As they were walking along the road, a man said to him, "I will follow you wherever you go."

58 Jesus replied, "Foxes have dens and birds have nests, but the Son of Man has no place to lay his head."

59 He said to another man, "Follow me."

But he replied, "Lord, first let me go and bury my father."

60 Jesus said to him, "Let the dead bury their own dead, but you go and proclaim the kingdom of God."

61 Still another said, "I will follow you, Lord; but first let me go back and say goodbye to my family."

62 Jesus replied, "No one who puts a hand to the plow and looks back is fit for service in the kingdom of God."

Luke 14:26 (NIV)

26 "If anyone comes to me and does not hate father and mother, wife and children, brothers and sisters—yes, even their own life—such a person cannot be my disciple."

✞ GOD'S PLAN FOR EVANGELISM AND DISCIPLESHIP ✞

Prospective believers should be so committed to God and following his plan that when they find out how to obtain eternal life they should be willing to give up all that they have and are doing to work their own plan, and instead to follow God's plan. Eternal life is like the treasure hidden in a field and the fine pearl that was found as presented in Jesus' parables. Eternal life is worth giving up everything our temporal lives can offer.

Matthew 13:44-46 (NIV)

[44] "The kingdom of heaven is like treasure hidden in a field. When a man found it, he hid it again, and then in his joy went and sold all he had and bought that field.

[45] "Again, the kingdom of heaven is like a merchant looking for fine pearls. [46] When he found one of great value, he went away and sold everything he had and bought it."

DISCUSSION QUESTIONS

1. What should a prospective believer be willing to do to show his commitment to God and to obtain eternal life?
2. Why is the offer of eternal life considered a temporary offer?

✟ GOD'S PLAN FOR EVANGELISM AND DISCIPLESHIP ✟

REPENTANCE

repent[1]

1. to feel such sorrow for sin or fault as to be disposed to change one's life for the better; be penitent

penitent

1. feeling or expressing sorrow for sin or wrongdoing and disposed to atonement and amendment; repentant; contrite

Repentance is turning from working your own plan to working God's plan. For unbelievers working your own plan means working any plan but God's plan. It usually has to do with some self-interest: career, money, hobbies, good works, etc. These are not bad plans but only God's plan leads to eternal life. The bible says that when Jesus called his first disciples they left their businesses to follow him. They believed that he was the Messiah and were willing to repent of what they were doing to learn God's plan as taught by Jesus. These were hard working men who heard Jesus talk about eternal life, and the need to repent and believe the good news and they decided that that was what they wanted and believed that Jesus knew the plan to get there. I believe that today Jesus wants his Ambassadors to study and to know him and obey him, repenting of all things that are against and not according to God's plan.

Matthew 4:18-20 (NIV)

[18] As Jesus was walking beside the Sea of Galilee, he saw two brothers, Simon called Peter and his brother Andrew. They were casting a net into the lake, for they were fishermen. [19] "Come, follow me," Jesus said, "and I will send you out to

✠ GOD'S PLAN FOR EVANGELISM AND DISCIPLESHIP ✠

fish for people." [20] At once they left their nets and followed him.

Mark 1:14-15 (NIV)

[14] After John was put in prison, Jesus went into Galilee, proclaiming the good news of God. [15] "The time has come," he said. "The kingdom of God has come near. Repent and believe the good news!"

Matthew 4:17 (NIV)

[17] From that time on Jesus began to preach, "Repent, for the kingdom of heaven has come near."

Jesus knows how important material possessions mean to people. People worry about having enough no matter how large or small amounts they have. Some people have financial plans to help them to retire and live a life of leisure. This is not God's plan. God expects us to work for him our entire lives. The problem is not in saving money but in being self-serving. God wants us to use our financial resources to meet our own financial needs and to work God's plan. God knows our financial needs and will meet them. He wants us to have our priorities in the correct order. He wants us first to work God's plan and then have faith that he will continue to meet our daily financial needs. He wants us to focus on knowing where our true treasure is and to keep working God's plan to increase our eternal rewards.

Luke 12:16-21 (NIV)

[16] And he told them this parable: "The ground of a certain rich man yielded an abundant harvest. [17] He thought to himself, 'What shall I do? I have no place to store my crops.'

¹⁸ "Then he said, 'This is what I'll do. I will tear down my barns and build bigger ones, and there I will store my surplus grain. ¹⁹ And I'll say to myself, "You have plenty of grain laid up for many years. Take life easy; eat, drink and be merry."'

²⁰ "But God said to him, 'You fool! This very night your life will be demanded from you. Then who will get what you have prepared for yourself?'

²¹ "This is how it will be with whoever stores up things for themselves but is not rich toward God."

Matthew 6:19-34 (NIV)

¹⁹ "Do not store up for yourselves treasures on earth, where moths and vermin destroy, and where thieves break in and steal. ²⁰ But store up for yourselves treasures in heaven, where moths and vermin do not destroy, and where thieves do not break in and steal. ²¹ For where your treasure is, there your heart will be also.

²² "The eye is the lamp of the body. If your eyes are healthy,[a] your whole body will be full of light. ²³ But if your eyes are unhealthy,[b] your whole body will be full of darkness. If then the light within you is darkness, how great is that darkness!

²⁴ "No one can serve two masters. Either you will hate the one and love the other, or you will be devoted to the one and despise the other. You cannot serve both God and money.

²⁵ "Therefore I tell you, do not worry about your life, what you will eat or drink; or about your body, what you will wear. Is not life more than food, and the body more than clothes? ²⁶ Look at the birds of the air; they do not sow or reap or store away in barns, and yet your heavenly Father feeds them. Are you not much more valuable than they? ²⁷ Can any one of you by worrying add a single hour to your life[c]?

✠ GOD'S PLAN FOR EVANGELISM AND DISCIPLESHIP ✠

28 "And why do you worry about clothes? See how the flowers of the field grow. They do not labor or spin. 29 Yet I tell you that not even Solomon in all his splendor was dressed like one of these. 30 If that is how God clothes the grass of the field, which is here today and tomorrow is thrown into the fire, will he not much more clothe you—you of little faith? 31 So do not worry, saying, 'What shall we eat?' or 'What shall we drink?' or 'What shall we wear?' 32 For the pagans run after all these things, and your heavenly Father knows that you need them. 33 But seek first his kingdom and his righteousness, and all these things will be given to you as well. 34 Therefore do not worry about tomorrow, for tomorrow will worry about itself. Each day has enough trouble of its own."

DISCUSSION QUESTIONS

1. What is man's plan?
2. What is God's plan?
3. In light of questions 1 and 2, what is repentance?

✝ GOD'S PLAN FOR EVANGELISM AND DISCIPLESHIP ✝

FAITH

faith
1.
confidence or trust in a person or thing:
faith in another's ability.
2.
belief in God or in the doctrines or teachings of religion:
the firm faith of the Pilgrims.
3.
belief in anything, as a code of ethics, standards of merit, etc.:
to be of the same faith with someone concerning honesty.
4.
a system of religious belief:
the Christian faith; the Jewish faith.

Eternal life is by grace through faith in Jesus Christ. By grace God is responsible to makes the gospel message clear to the unbeliever and then by faith it's man's responsibility to makes a decision to accept or reject the gospel message.

By grace God is the one who reveals, enables, and draws God's gospel message to the unbeliever. The gospel message is that Jesus is the Messiah who died on the cross in our place to deliver us from sin so that we could have eternal life with God. Not everyone who hears the message is ready to accept it. Ambassadors are to share the message with as many people as possible because Ambassadors are unable to judge whether God has made a person ready or not. An Ambassador can only judge by the decision that the unbeliever makes; i.e. whether the unbeliever accepts or rejects the message.

✟ GOD'S PLAN FOR EVANGELISM AND DISCIPLESHIP ✟

Luke 10:21 (NIV)

²¹ At that time Jesus, full of joy through the Holy Spirit, said, "I praise you, Father, Lord of heaven and earth, because you have hidden these things from the wise and learned, and revealed them to little children. Yes, Father, for this is what you were pleased to do."

John 6:60-65 (NIV)

⁶⁰ On hearing it, many of his disciples said, "This is a hard teaching. Who can accept it?"

⁶¹ Aware that his disciples were grumbling about this, Jesus said to them, "Does this offend you? ⁶² Then what if you see the Son of Man ascend to where he was before! ⁶³ The Spirit gives life; the flesh counts for nothing. The words I have spoken to you—they are full of the Spirit[a] and life. ⁶⁴ Yet there are some of you who do not believe." For Jesus had known from the beginning which of them did not believe and who would betray him. ⁶⁵ He went on to say, "This is why I told you that no one can come to me unless the Father has enabled them."

John 6:44 (NIV)

⁴⁴ "No one can come to me unless the Father who sent me draws them, and I will raise them up at the last day."

After the gospel message has been shared with the unbeliever the Ambassador should be ready to answer any questions the unbeliever may have and lead the unbeliever to faith in Jesus. Eternal life is by grace through faith in Jesus Christ. How does an unbeliever express their faith in Jesus? Many make a profession of faith through prayer. A prayer of faith in Jesus can be as simple as:

Heavenly Father,

I believe that your son Jesus is the Messiah who died on the cross in my place so that I may have eternal life with you. I accept your free gift and give my life to you to teach me how to live life according to your plan. Amen.

Anyone who sincerely says this prayer becomes a Christian and should immediately join a group of fellow Ambassadors who are following God's plan. Jesus' first Ambassadors joined his group and he taught them God's plan for the three plus years of his earthly ministry. But it all began with God's grace, followed by acceptance of the gospel message through faith. Then discipleship is the natural next step in living life according to God's plan.

Jesus made several promises that said everyone who believed in him would have eternal life. We can believe in those promises because Jesus has kept all of God's promises which proves that he is the Messiah.

John 3:16 (NIV)

[16] For God so loved the world that he gave his one and only Son, that whoever believes in him shall not perish but have eternal life.

John 5:24 (NIV)

[24] Very truly I tell you, whoever hears my word and believes him who sent me has eternal life and will not be judged but has crossed over from death to life.

John 6:40 (NIV)

⁴⁰ For my Father's will is that everyone who looks to the Son and believes in him shall have eternal life, and I will raise them up at the last day.

John 6:47 (NIV)

⁴⁷ Very truly I tell you, the one who believes has eternal life.

DISCUSSION QUESTIONS

1. Why is an unbeliever able to understand the gospel message when it is shared with him?
2. What should an Ambassador do after the unbeliever says a prayer of faith?

✟ GOD'S PLAN FOR EVANGELISM AND DISCIPLESHIP ✟

BAPTISM

Baptism is important to Jesus. During his ministry Jesus and his Ambassadors went into the Judean countryside and baptized. Jesus himself did not baptize anyone, but his Ambassadors did. At the end of his ministry Jesus gave some last instructions to his Ambassadors. He commanded them to make Ambassadors of all nations and to baptize them in the name of the Father and the Son, and the Holy Spirit.

Baptism is an outward sign where the new Ambassadors expresses his commitment to repent of his own plan and to follow God's plan. The actual baptism is with water where the new Ambassador stands in the water so as to identify with Jesus' death on the cross, gets dipped into the water to identify with Jesus' burial, and then gets lifted out of the water to identify with Jesus's resurrection from the dead.

New Ambassadors should be baptized as soon as possible in obedience to Jesus' command to be baptized.

John 3:22 (NIV)

[22] After this, Jesus and his disciples went out into the Judean countryside, where he spent some time with them, and baptized.

John 4:1-2 (NIV)

[1] Now Jesus learned that the Pharisees had heard that he was gaining and baptizing more disciples than John— [2] although in fact it was not Jesus who baptized, but his disciples.

Matthew 28:18-20 (NIV)

[18] Then Jesus came to them and said, "All authority in heaven and on earth has been given to me. [19] Therefore go and make disciples of all nations, baptizing them in the name of the Father and of the Son and of the Holy Spirit, [20] and teaching

them to obey everything I have commanded you. And surely I am with you always, to the very end of the age."

DISCUSSION QUESTIONS

1. What is the purpose of water baptism?
2. What does water baptism symbolize?

✝ GOD'S PLAN FOR EVANGELISM AND DISCIPLESHIP ✝

PRAYER

Prayer is talking with God and making your needs known to him.

Jesus said that we should remain in him and he will remain in us. Remaining in him means trusting and obeying God's plan. Jesus says that he will remain in us, working through us producing the fruit he desires. God will work through us if we trust and obey his plan. If we do our part, he will do his part, and whatever we ask for in prayer will be given to us. So that is the key to answered prayer trusting and obeying God's plan. If we trust and obey our own plan Jesus says that it will be like a branch that is cut off and thrown away and withers because it did not allow the life giving power of the Holy Spirit to flow through them. Those withered branches are like people who did not trust and obey God's plan and on judgment day they will be thrown into the fire of hell for all eternity.

John 15:4-16 (NIV)

[4] Remain in me, as I also remain in you. No branch can bear fruit by itself; it must remain in the vine. Neither can you bear fruit unless you remain in me.

[5] "I am the vine; you are the branches. If you remain in me and I in you, you will bear much fruit; apart from me you can do nothing. [6] If you do not remain in me, you are like a branch that is thrown away and withers; such branches are picked up, thrown into the fire and burned. [7] If you remain in me and my words remain in you, ask whatever you wish, and it will be done for you. [8] This is to my Father's glory, that you bear much fruit, showing yourselves to be my disciples.

[9] "As the Father has loved me, so have I loved you. Now remain in my love. [10] If you keep my commands, you will remain in my love, just as I have kept my Father's commands and remain in his love. [11] I have told you this so that my joy

may be in you and that your joy may be complete. ¹² My command is this: Love each other as I have loved you. ¹³ Greater love has no one than this: to lay down one's life for one's friends. ¹⁴ You are my friends if you do what I command. ¹⁵ I no longer call you servants, because a servant does not know his master's business. Instead, I have called you friends, for everything that I learned from my Father I have made known to you. ¹⁶ You did not choose me, but I chose you and appointed you so that you might go and bear fruit—fruit that will last—and so that whatever you ask in my name the Father will give you."

Jesus' Ambassadors asked him how to pray and he taught them a prayer that is commonly called The Lord's prayer. It's not meant to be a prayer that you recite but one that lets you know what needs can be asked for in prayer such as cares about daily needs, forgiveness, temptation, and many more needs.

Matthew 6:9-15 (NIV)

⁹ "This, then, is how you should pray:

"'Our Father in heaven,
hallowed be your name,
¹⁰ your kingdom come,
your will be done,
 on earth as it is in heaven.
¹¹ Give us today our daily bread.
¹² And forgive us our debts,
 as we also have forgiven our debtors.
¹³ And lead us not into temptation,[a]
but deliver us from the evil one.[b]'

¹⁴ For if you forgive other people when they sin against you, your heavenly Father will also forgive you. ¹⁵ But if you do not forgive others their sins, your Father will not forgive your sins.

The bible says that Jesus spent time alone in prayer. With all the activity happening all around him and his Ambassadors Jesus would still find time to be alone in prayer. Early morning when it was still dark was his best time for prayer. Today Ambassadors should find their best time to pray where they can be alone, in a quiet place, and where they will not be interrupted. But Jesus said there are times when Ambassadors should pray together with other Ambassadors. He said when two or more pray together that he would be there with them and that when they agree in prayer that the Father will do whatever they asked for. Of course that prayer would have to be in agreement with God's will.

Mark 1:35 (NIV)

[35] Very early in the morning, while it was still dark, Jesus got up, left the house and went off to a solitary place, where he prayed.

Matthew 18:19-20 (NIV)

[19] "Again, truly I tell you that if two of you on earth agree about anything they ask for, it will be done for them by my Father in heaven. [20] For where two or three gather in my name, there am I with them."

Ambassadors should always listen to God, try to discern the will of God, and pray that his will be done.

Matthew 26:42 (NIV)

[42] He went away a second time and prayed, "My Father, if it is not possible for this cup to be taken away unless I drink it, may your will be done."

Jesus taught his Ambassadors that they should be persistent in prayer and not give up when God does not answer their prayers after a short time has passed. With persistence sometimes God answers our prayers even after a long time has passed.

Luke 18:1-8 (NIV)

¹ Then Jesus told his disciples a parable to show them that they should always pray and not give up. ² He said: "In a certain town there was a judge who neither feared God nor cared what people thought. ³ And there was a widow in that town who kept coming to him with the plea, 'Grant me justice against my adversary.'

⁴ "For some time he refused. But finally he said to himself, 'Even though I don't fear God or care what people think, ⁵ yet because this widow keeps bothering me, I will see that she gets justice, so that she won't eventually come and attack me!'"

⁶ And the Lord said, "Listen to what the unjust judge says. ⁷ And will not God bring about justice for his chosen ones, who cry out to him day and night? Will he keep putting them off? ⁸ I tell you, he will see that they get justice, and quickly. However, when the Son of Man comes, will he find faith on the earth?"

Sometimes when we have an immediate need God likes it when we are bold in our prayers. He likes when we don't give up seeking answers to our prayers. It may feel as if we are nagging God but he likes it when we keep asking until we receive.

Luke 11:5-13 (NIV)

⁵ Then Jesus said to them, "Suppose you have a friend, and you go to him at midnight and say, 'Friend, lend me three loaves of bread; ⁶ a friend of mine on a journey has come to me, and I have no food to offer him.' ⁷ And suppose the one inside answers, 'Don't bother me. The door is already locked, and my children and I are in bed. I can't get up and give you anything.'

⁸ I tell you, even though he will not get up and give you the bread because of friendship, yet because of your shameless audacity[a] he will surely get up and give you as much as you need.

⁹ "So I say to you: Ask and it will be given to you; seek and you will find; knock and the door will be opened to you. ¹⁰ For everyone who asks receives; the one who seeks finds; and to the one who knocks, the door will be opened.

¹¹ "Which of you fathers, if your son asks for[b] a fish, will give him a snake instead? ¹² Or if he asks for an egg, will give him a scorpion? ¹³ If you then, though you are evil, know how to give good gifts to your children, how much more will your Father in heaven give the Holy Spirit to those who ask him!"

DISCUSSION QUESTIONS

1. What is important to having answered prayer?
2. How should the Lord's Prayer be used?
3. What should we do when God does not answer our prayer right away?

COMMUNION

Communion is the coming together and taking of the bread and wine to symbolize the price that Jesus paid on the cross. The bread represents Jesus' body which suffered much during his crucifixion. The wine represents Jesus' blood which was poured out for many for the forgiveness of sins. Ambassadors should observe this celebration eat the bread and drink the wine often to remind us of the price that was paid which brought salvation.

Matthew 26:26-29 (NIV)

[6] While they were eating, Jesus took bread, and when he had given thanks, he broke it and gave it to his disciples, saying, "Take and eat; this is my body."

[27] Then he took a cup, and when he had given thanks, he gave it to them, saying, "Drink from it, all of you. [28] This is my blood of the[a] covenant, which is poured out for many for the forgiveness of sins. [29] I tell you, I will not drink from this fruit of the vine from now on until that day when I drink it new with you in my Father's kingdom."

DISCUSSION QUESTIONS

1. When we take communion what are we sharing in common?

TEACHING

Jesus taught on various subjects and most of these subjects have been included in the various categories in this book discussing who, what, when, and why of the subject. This category on Teaching discusses who and where.

Jesus taught in the synagogues, the temple courts, near the lake, and the countryside, and just about anywhere when discussing subjects privately with his Ambassadors.

Many times the bible speaks of Jesus teaching in their synagogues on the Sabbath when they were outside of Jerusalem.

Matthew 4:23 (NIV)

23 Jesus went throughout Galilee, teaching in their synagogues, proclaiming the good news of the kingdom, and healing every disease and sickness among the people.

When he was in Jerusalem he would teach in the temple courts.

John 7:14-16 (NIV)

14 Not until halfway through the festival did Jesus go up to the temple courts and begin to teach. 15 The Jews there were amazed and asked, "How did this man get such learning without having been taught?"

16 Jesus answered, "My teaching is not my own. It comes from the one who sent me."

✞ GOD'S PLAN FOR EVANGELISM AND DISCIPLESHIP ✞

When teaching to crowds of people Jesus spoke at the Lake near the house and in the countryside. He spoke to the crowds using parables.

Matthew 13:34 (NIV)

³⁴ Jesus spoke all these things to the crowd in parables; he did not say anything to them without using a parable.

Mark 2:13 (NIV)

¹³ Once again Jesus went out beside the lake. A large crowd came to him, and he began to teach them.

The disciples were a small group of twelve and there were times when Jesus taught them in private and away from the crowds. He taught them in plain language, but he taught the crowds in parables.

Matthew 17:19 (NIV)

¹⁹ Then the disciples came to Jesus in private and asked, "Why couldn't we drive it out?"

Mark 4:10-11 (NIV)

¹⁰ When he was alone, the Twelve and the others around him asked him about the parables. ¹¹ He told them, "The secret of the kingdom of God has been given to you. But to those on the outside everything is said in parables."

DISCUSSION QUESTIONS

1. When in a small group of disciples what kind of language should Ambassadors teach them with?
2. When in a very large audience of believers and unbelievers what kind of language should Ambassadors teach them with?

FELLOWSHIP - UNITY

Jesus spoke of the unity and oneness he has with the Father and his Ambassadors. Although Jesus and the Father are different persons they share a unity and the same nature. Only the Father and the Son know each other, plus those to whom Jesus has chosen to reveal him.

Matthew 11:27 (NIV)

27 "All things have been committed to me by my Father. No one knows the Son except the Father, and no one knows the Father except the Son and those to whom the Son chooses to reveal him."

One demonstration that the Father and Jesus are united is the miracles that Jesus does in the Father's name. Another demonstration of this unity is that the Ambassadors cannot be taken out of Jesus' or the Father's hand. Jesus stated very clearly that he and the Father are one.

John 10:25-30 (NIV)

25 Jesus answered, "I did tell you, but you do not believe. The works I do in my Father's name testify about me, 26 but you do not believe because you are not my sheep. 27 My sheep listen to my voice; I know them, and they follow me. 28 I give them eternal life, and they shall never perish; no one will snatch them out of my hand. 29 My Father, who has given them to me, is greater than all[a]; no one can snatch them out of my Father's hand. 30 I and the Father are one."

Ambassadors know the Father because they know Jesus. The more we get to know Jesus through studying his words and works in the bible and obeying God's plan, the more we will grow to know the Father. To be the best Ambassadors of God we can be we need to know him so that we can then properly represent him.

Ambassadors can know the Holy Spirit because after Pentecost he has lived within us not just with us. This is an intimate growing relationship as we yield to him and what he reveals to us through the word of God. So there is unity and oneness between God the Father, God the Son, and God the Holy Spirit. This unity and oneness is seen in what happened when John the Baptist baptized Jesus. In Matthew 3:16-17 all three persons of God are actively present, thus giving us a picture of the doctrine of the Trinity describing the One God existing in Three persons and still being the same in nature.

Matthew 3:16-17 (NIV)

^{16} As soon as Jesus was baptized, he went up out of the water. At that moment heaven was opened, and he saw the Spirit of God descending like a dove and alighting on him. ^{17} And a voice from heaven said, "This is my Son, whom I love; with him I am well pleased."

All Ambassadors that are obeying God's plan are in unity with each other as brothers and sisters in the Lord.

Mark 3:33-35 (NIV)

^{33} "Who are my mother and my brothers?" he asked.

^{34} Then he looked at those seated in a circle around him and said, "Here are my mother and my brothers! ^{35} Whoever does God's will is my brother and sister and mother."

Jesus said that those who the sow seeds of the gospel today are working together with those who reap the harvest tomorrow. Both sowing and reaping are important to bringing souls to salvation so there is teamwork going on and teamwork requires a unity of purpose through the opportunities we are given.

John 4:36-38 (NIV)

[36] Even now the one who reaps draws a wage and harvests a crop for eternal life, so that the sower and the reaper may be glad together. [37] Thus the saying 'One sows and another reaps' is true. [38] I sent you to reap what you have not worked for. Others have done the hard work, and you have reaped the benefits of their labor."

Ambassadors should be inclusive of other Ambassadors who are working God's plan even if those Ambassadors are not a part of their group. All Ambassadors are in unity if they are working effectively God's plan.

Mark 9:38-40 (NIV)

[38] "Teacher," said John, "we saw someone driving out demons in your name and we told him to stop, because he was not one of us."

[39] "Do not stop him," Jesus said. "For no one who does a miracle in my name can in the next moment say anything bad about me, [40] for whoever is not against us is for us."

✞ GOD'S PLAN FOR EVANGELISM AND DISCIPLESHIP ✞

DISCUSSION QUESTIONS

1. What is one evidence that the Father and Jesus are united?
2. How do Ambassadors get to know the Father, Jesus, and the Holy Spirit?
3. How are Ambassadors united together with each other?

FELLOWSHIP - POWER

The twelve disciples were granted power by Jesus to drive out demons and to cure diseases when they were being sent out to preach the kingdom of God.

Matthew 10:1 (NIV)

[1] Jesus called his twelve disciples to him and gave them authority to drive out impure spirits and to heal every disease and sickness.

Later before returning to heaven he told his disciples to "stay in the city until you have been clothed with power on high."

Luke 24:49 (NIV)

[49] I am going to send you what my Father has promised; but stay in the city until you have been clothed with power from on high."

The Holy Spirit of God has been given to Ambassadors so that they can share in the Holy Spirit's power to perform the work that the Father wants.

DISCUSSION QUESTIONS

1. What does the power of the Holy Spirit allow Ambassadors to perform?

FELLOWSHIP - STEWARDSHIP

Stewardship - the position and duties of a steward; a person who acts as the surrogate of another or others, especially by managing property, financial affairs, an estate, etc.

Ambassadors are stewards of God's resources.

Ambassadors should manage the resources that God has given us in order to be fruitful. God will give us resources according to our abilities. At the proper time God will come back to judge our stewardship. For those who have shared God's resources and have been fruitful in gaining more than what they were given, God will reward them. For those who have not shared God's resources then they will be punished in hell for not being fruitful.

Matthew 25:14-30 (NIV)

[14] "Again, it will be like a man going on a journey, who called his servants and entrusted his wealth to them. [15] To one he gave five bags of gold, to another two bags, and to another one bag,[a] each according to his ability. Then he went on his journey. [16] The man who had received five bags of gold went at once and put his money to work and gained five bags more. [17] So also, the one with two bags of gold gained two more. [18] But the man who had received one bag went off, dug a hole in the ground and hid his master's money.

[19] "After a long time the master of those servants returned and settled accounts with them. [20] The man who had received five bags of gold brought the other five. 'Master,' he said, 'you entrusted me with five bags of gold. See, I have gained five more.'

[21] "His master replied, 'Well done, good and faithful servant! You have been faithful with a few things; I will put you in

charge of many things. Come and share your master's happiness!'

²² "The man with two bags of gold also came. 'Master,' he said, 'you entrusted me with two bags of gold; see, I have gained two more.'

²³ "His master replied, 'Well done, good and faithful servant! You have been faithful with a few things; I will put you in charge of many things. Come and share your master's happiness!'

²⁴ "Then the man who had received one bag of gold came. 'Master,' he said, 'I knew that you are a hard man, harvesting where you have not sown and gathering where you have not scattered seed. ²⁵ So I was afraid and went out and hid your gold in the ground. See, here is what belongs to you.'

²⁶ "His master replied, 'You wicked, lazy servant! So you knew that I harvest where I have not sown and gather where I have not scattered seed? ²⁷ Well then, you should have put my money on deposit with the bankers, so that when I returned I would have received it back with interest.

²⁸ "'So take the bag of gold from him and give it to the one who has ten bags. ²⁹ For whoever has will be given more, and they will have an abundance. Whoever does not have, even what they have will be taken from them. ³⁰ And throw that worthless servant outside, into the darkness, where there will be weeping and gnashing of teeth.'"

Jesus said that some wealthy Ambassadors make their contributions to the offering from their wealth and some Ambassadors make their contributions from the money that they have to live on. Jesus acknowledged that those who make their contributions from the latter will get special recognition because of their sacrificial giving.

Luke 21:1-4 (NIV)

¹ As Jesus looked up, he saw the rich putting their gifts into the temple treasury. ² He also saw a poor widow put in two very small copper coins. ³ "Truly I tell you," he said, "this poor widow has put in more than all the others. ⁴ All these people gave their gifts out of their wealth; but she out of her poverty put in all she had to live on."

Jesus taught his Ambassadors to love and take pity on neighbors who have fallen on hard times. Share with them the love of God that we would like other Ambassadors to share with us. We are to meet their immediate needs using our time, talent, and financial resources.

Luke 10:27-37 (NIV)

²⁷ He answered, "'Love the Lord your God with all your heart and with all your soul and with all your strength and with all your mind'[a]; and, 'Love your neighbor as yourself.'[b]"

²⁸ "You have answered correctly," Jesus replied. "Do this and you will live."

²⁹ But he wanted to justify himself, so he asked Jesus, "And who is my neighbor?"

³⁰ In reply Jesus said: "A man was going down from Jerusalem to Jericho, when he was attacked by robbers. They stripped him of his clothes, beat him and went away, leaving him half dead. ³¹ A priest happened to be going down the same road, and when he saw the man, he passed by on the other side. ³² So too, a Levite, when he came to the place and saw him, passed by on the other side. ³³ But a Samaritan, as he traveled, came where the man was; and when he saw him, he took pity on him. ³⁴ He went to him and bandaged his wounds, pouring on oil and wine. Then he put the man on his own donkey, brought him to an inn and took care of him. ³⁵ The next day he took out two

denarii[c] and gave them to the innkeeper. 'Look after him,' he said, 'and when I return, I will reimburse you for any extra expense you may have.'

³⁶ "Which of these three do you think was a neighbor to the man who fell into the hands of robbers?"

³⁷ The expert in the law replied, "The one who had mercy on him."

Jesus told him, "Go and do likewise."

DISCUSSION QUESTIONS

1. What type of investments should an Ambassador make in order be fruitful and be rewarded by God?
2. Why did Jesus give credit to the poor widow for putting in a large percentage of all she had?
3. How can Ambassadors show pity on those in need?

REPRODUCTION - CALLING

The calling is when after sharing the gospel with someone you ask him to accept Jesus as his Savior and Lord. Some people do not accept Jesus the first time they are called; and sometimes people do not continue to follow Jesus after they have made their first acceptance decision. Sometimes people walk away from following Jesus and go back to doing whatever they were doing before they made the initial acceptance decision.

The first four disciples, Peter, Andrew, John, and James did not follow Jesus permanently the first time they met him or received their first call. Andrew and John, in their first meeting with Jesus, asked if they could spend some time with him and he let them. Andrew found his brother Peter and introduced him to Jesus.

John 1:35-42 (NIV)

[35] The next day John was there again with two of his disciples. [36] When he saw Jesus passing by, he said, "Look, the Lamb of God!"

[37] When the two disciples heard him say this, they followed Jesus. [38] Turning around, Jesus saw them following and asked, "What do you want?"

They said, "Rabbi" (which means "Teacher"), "where are you staying?"

[39] "Come," he replied, "and you will see."

So they went and saw where he was staying, and they spent that day with him. It was about four in the afternoon.

⁴⁰ Andrew, Simon Peter's brother, was one of the two who heard what John had said and who had followed Jesus. ⁴¹ The first thing Andrew did was to find his brother Simon and tell him, "We have found the Messiah" (that is, the Christ). ⁴² And he brought him to Jesus.

Jesus looked at him and said, "You are Simon, son of John. You will be called Cephas" (which, when translated, is Peter[a]).

In a second call Peter, Andrew, John, and James were doing their work as fishermen and Jesus asked them to follow him and they immediately left their nets and followed him.

Matthew 4:18-22 (NIV)

¹⁸ As Jesus was walking beside the Sea of Galilee, he saw two brothers, Simon called Peter and his brother Andrew. They were casting a net into the lake, for they were fishermen. ¹⁹ "Come, follow me," Jesus said, "and I will send you out to fish for people." ²⁰ At once they left their nets and followed him.

²¹ Going on from there, he saw two other brothers, James son of Zebedee and his brother John. They were in a boat with their father Zebedee, preparing their nets. Jesus called them, ²² and immediately they left the boat and their father and followed him.

They went with Jesus as he was "teaching in synagogues, preaching the good news of the kingdom, and healing every disease and sickness among the people." Later on they returned to their fishing business.

The third time they were called they stayed with him permanently. They were washing their nets after a mostly unproductive day of fishing when Jesus asked them to "Put out into deep water, and let down the nets for a catch" (Lk 5:4). They did and caught such a large catch of fish that their nets began to break and the boats began to sink. Peter and the others were astonished at the catch. "Then Jesus said to Simon, 'Don't be afraid; from now on you will catch men.' So they pulled their boats up on shore, left everything and followed him". This time Jesus helped the disciples when they had a personal need and that made a big difference in how committed they became to him and to following God's plan.

Luke 5:1-11 (NIV)

¹ One day as Jesus was standing by the Lake of Gennesaret,[a] the people were crowding around him and listening to the word of God. ² He saw at the water's edge two boats, left there by the fishermen, who were washing their nets. ³ He got into one of the boats, the one belonging to Simon, and asked him to put out a little from shore. Then he sat down and taught the people from the boat.

⁴ When he had finished speaking, he said to Simon, "Put out into deep water, and let down the nets for a catch."

⁵ Simon answered, "Master, we've worked hard all night and haven't caught anything. But because you say so, I will let down the nets."

⁶ When they had done so, they caught such a large number of fish that their nets began to break. ⁷ So they signaled their partners in the other boat to come and help them, and they came and filled both boats so full that they began to sink.

⁸ When Simon Peter saw this, he fell at Jesus' knees and said, "Go away from me, Lord; I am a sinful man!" ⁹ For he and all his companions were astonished at the catch of fish they had taken, ¹⁰ and so were James and John, the sons of Zebedee, Simon's partners.

Then Jesus said to Simon, "Don't be afraid; from now on you will fish for people." [11] So they pulled their boats up on shore, left everything and followed him.

People have various reactions to the calling. One reaction is that they reject it for lack of understanding; another reaction is that they accept it with joy but because they do not get grounded in the basics of God's plan they fall away when trouble or persecution comes; another reaction is that they accept it but they allow their own plan to lead them into not following God's plan and they become unfruitful; but the reaction that pleases God and leads to eternal life is the reaction where the Ambassador hears the gospel, accepts Jesus as his Savior and Lord, and joins a discipleship group and gets discipled to the point where they are sharing God's plan with others and discipling them to where there is a multiplication of effort and results.

Matthew 13:3-8 (NIV)

[3] Then he told them many things in parables, saying: "A farmer went out to sow his seed. [4] As he was scattering the seed, some fell along the path, and the birds came and ate it up. [5] Some fell on rocky places, where it did not have much soil. It sprang up quickly, because the soil was shallow. [6] But when the sun came up, the plants were scorched, and they withered because they had no root. [7] Other seed fell among thorns, which grew up and choked the plants. [8] Still other seed fell on good soil, where it produced a crop—a hundred, sixty or thirty times what was sown.

Matthew 13:18-23 (NIV)

[18] "Listen then to what the parable of the sower means: [19] When anyone hears the message about the kingdom and does not understand it, the evil one comes and snatches away what was sown in their heart. This is the seed sown along the path. [20] The

seed falling on rocky ground refers to someone who hears the word and at once receives it with joy. [21] But since they have no root, they last only a short time. When trouble or persecution comes because of the word, they quickly fall away. [22] The seed falling among the thorns refers to someone who hears the word, but the worries of this life and the deceitfulness of wealth choke the word, making it unfruitful. [23] But the seed falling on good soil refers to someone who hears the word and understands it. This is the one who produces a crop, yielding a hundred, sixty or thirty times what was sown."

✝ GOD'S PLAN FOR EVANGELISM AND DISCIPLESHIP ✝

DISCUSSION QUESTIONS

1. What reactions to the gospel lead to unfruitfulness?
2. What reactions to the gospel lead to fruitfulness?
3. What does it mean to produce a crop, yielding a hundred, sixty or thirty times what was sown?

REPRODUCTION - APPOINTMENT

Hundreds of people followed Jesus from place to place. From this large group Jesus appointed twelve disciples to the position of apostles. The term apostle has a similar meaning to the term Ambassador; i.e., messenger or authorized representative. They were chosen by Jesus to be his inner circle and to receive a more intense training spending more time closely with him.

Mark 3:13-15 (NIV)

[13] Jesus went up on a mountainside and called to him those he wanted, and they came to him. [14] He appointed twelve[a] that they might be with him and that he might send them out to preach [15] and to have authority to drive out demons.

Before making his appointments Jesus spent a night praying to God. This task of making the appointments was to be very important because it would be from the twelve apostles that Jesus would began his church. The apostles were there when the Holy Spirit came at Pentecost baptizing them in the Holy Spirit and with power so that they could grow the early church.

Luke 6:12-13 (NIV)

[12] One of those days Jesus went out to a mountainside to pray, and spent the night praying to God. [13] When morning came, he called his disciples to him and chose twelve of them, whom he also designated apostles:

The apostles were a group of ordinary men with diverse backgrounds. The one personality trait that they had which was very important to following Jesus was obedience.

Today, from a large group of disciples, the leader should pick a small number of Ambassadors to spend more time with them. The leader should take this group with him when he goes out sharing God's plan so that they could learn from example what an Ambassador should do.

DISCUSSION QUESTIONS

1. What are the similar meanings to the terms apostle and Ambassador?
2. What was the most common personality trait that the apostles shared?

✝ GOD'S PLAN FOR EVANGELISM AND DISCIPLESHIP ✝

REPRODUCTION - DELEGATION

Jesus delegated or sent out the twelve apostles with the responsibility to share the gospel with the authority and power to drive out evil spirits and to heal every disease and sickness. Their message was that the kingdom of heaven is near. They were sent out two by two for six teams of two. Jesus could have sent them out by themselves by ones and covered more ground but then the apostles would not have had the fellowship that is needed to support each other especially in adverse situations.

Jesus sent them out with a principle to guide them "Freely you have received, freely give." (Mat 10:8) Since God has been so generous with us we should be generous with others. Another principle that Jesus gave them was that if you run into people who are not open to your message then to move on to another person. Jesus said, "If anyone will not welcome you or listen to your words, shake the dust off your feet when you leave that home or town" (Mat 10:14). As far as people accepting or not accepting your message remember the adage, "Some will. Some won't. Next."

Tough situations were bound to occur and Jesus gave the apostles this admonition, "I am sending you out like sheep among wolves. Therefore be as shrewd as snakes and as innocent as doves." (Mat 10:16)

Matthew 10:1 (NIV)

¹ Jesus called his twelve disciples to him and gave them authority to drive out impure spirits and to heal every disease and sickness.

Matthew 10:5-16 (NIV)

⁵ These twelve Jesus sent out with the following instructions: "Do not go among the Gentiles or enter any town of the

✞ GOD'S PLAN FOR EVANGELISM AND DISCIPLESHIP ✞

Samaritans. ⁶ Go rather to the lost sheep of Israel. ⁷ As you go, proclaim this message: 'The kingdom of heaven has come near.' ⁸ Heal the sick, raise the dead, cleanse those who have leprosy,[a] drive out demons. Freely you have received; freely give.

⁹ "Do not get any gold or silver or copper to take with you in your belts— ¹⁰ no bag for the journey or extra shirt or sandals or a staff, for the worker is worth his keep. ¹¹ Whatever town or village you enter, search there for some worthy person and stay at their house until you leave. ¹² As you enter the home, give it your greeting. ¹³ If the home is deserving, let your peace rest on it; if it is not, let your peace return to you. ¹⁴ If anyone will not welcome you or listen to your words, leave that home or town and shake the dust off your feet. ¹⁵ Truly I tell you, it will be more bearable for Sodom and Gomorrah on the Day of Judgment than for that town.

¹⁶ "I am sending you out like sheep among wolves. Therefore be as shrewd as snakes and as innocent as doves.

Jesus also sent out seventy-two others with the message that "the kingdom of God is near you." They were sent out ahead of Jesus to every town and place where he was about to go. Jesus wanted to reach as many people as possible because there were a lot of people who had not heard the gospel yet. Jesus gave the same admonition to the seventy-two that he had given to the twelve and that is "I am sending you out like sheep among wolves."

Luke 10:1-3 (NIV)

¹ After this the Lord appointed seventy-two[a] others and sent them two by two ahead of him to every town and place where he was about to go. ² He told them, "The harvest is plentiful, but the workers are few. Ask the Lord of the harvest, therefore, to send out workers into his harvest field. ³ Go! I am sending you out like lambs among wolves.

Luke 10:9-12 (NIV)

⁹ Heal the sick who are there and tell them, 'The kingdom of God has come near to you.' ¹⁰ But when you enter a town and are not welcomed, go into its streets and say, ¹¹ 'Even the dust of your town we wipe from our feet as a warning to you. Yet be sure of this: The kingdom of God has come near.' ¹² I tell you, it will be more bearable on that day for Sodom than for that town.

DISCUSSION QUESTIONS

1. What does it mean to be delegated?
2. What does it mean to be sent out like "lambs among wolves?"

REPRODUCTION - ACCOUNTABILITY

When the twelve apostles returned they reported to Jesus all that they had done and taught. With joy they reported their successes and victories.

Luke 9:10 (NIV)

¹⁰ When the apostles returned, they reported to Jesus what they had done. Then he took them with him and they withdrew by themselves to a town called Bethsaida.

When the seventy-two returned they reported to Jesus their victories over Satan and his demons. And Jesus rejoiced with them.

Luke 10:17-19 (NIV)

¹⁷ The seventy-two returned with joy and said, "Lord, even the demons submit to us in your name."

¹⁸ He replied, "I saw Satan fall like lightning from heaven. ¹⁹ I have given you authority to trample on snakes and scorpions and to overcome all the power of the enemy; nothing will harm you."

Today the Ambassadors who have been sent out two by two should return and report to the group how the Holy Spirit had helped them achieve victories; and also share some of the challenges they faced. Accountability is good for answering questions about productivity too. New ideas can be shared and discussed to generate synergy for more opportunities to reach the field of unbelievers who are ready to believe and become fruitful to God.

DISCUSSION QUESTIONS

1. Who was defeated by the seventy-two?
2. Who should Ambassadors aim their attacks at when trying to win spiritual battles?

REPRODUCTION - INCREASE

The more sowers and reapers there are the greater the chance of increase in the growth of the church. God is in control of the cutting back and pruning to increase the fruitfulness of the Ambassador. Jesus said, "The kingdom of heaven has been forcefully advancing, and forceful men lay hold of it." (Mat 11:12) When sower and reapers follow God's plan and persevere in their work then increase is going to come.

John 15:1-4 (NIV)

[1] "I am the true vine, and my Father is the gardener. [2] He cuts off every branch in me that bears no fruit, while every branch that does bear fruit he prunes[a] so that it will be even more fruitful. [3] You are already clean because of the word I have spoken to you. [4] Remain in me, as I also remain in you. No branch can bear fruit by itself; it must remain in the vine. Neither can you bear fruit unless you remain in me."

Jesus gave the parable of the mustard seed and the yeast to show how the church from its small beginnings was going to grow into a worldwide organization and movement.

Luke 13:18-21 (NIV)

[18] Then Jesus asked, "What is the kingdom of God like? What shall I compare it to? [19] It is like a mustard seed, which a man took and planted in his garden. It grew and became a tree, and the birds perched in its branches."

[20] Again he asked, "What shall I compare the kingdom of God to? [21] It is like yeast that a woman took and mixed into about sixty pounds[a] of flour until it worked all through the dough."

Today, using God's plan for sharing the Gospel multiplication is what is expected. Those who have been called, get appointed, then delegated; and held accountable for productiveness, then increase will occur and then the process repeats itself to where there is multiplication.

DISCUSSION QUESTIONS

1. How will increase through multiplication occur in the church?
2. When and where has multiplication of growth occurred in the church?

✞ GOD'S PLAN FOR EVANGELISM AND DISCIPLESHIP ✞

GOSPEL PRESENTATION

WHAT EVERYONE WANTS

- After death, everyone wants to go to heaven, especially considering the alternative, which is hell.

- Most people do not think too much about their eternal destiny, they are too busy living life.

- Jesus said that there is only one way to get to heaven and that is through putting their faith in him as Savior and Lord and then living according to God's plan.

- But one might ask, why do I have to do that? What's wrong with living according to my plan?

THE PROBLEM FOR UNBELIEVERS

- Everyone has a sin nature which causes us to sin.

- Unbelievers have a personal record book in which every sin that they have ever committed is recorded.

- On judgement day God looks at these sins and pronounces a guilty verdict.

- All guilty persons get sent to hell for all eternity.

NO PROBLEM FOR AMBASSADORS

- Ambassadors have a sin nature too, which causes them to sin.

- Ambassadors have a personal record book in which no sins are recorded because they have been forgiven.

- On judgement day God does not see any sins and pronounces an innocent verdict.

- All Ambassadors get sent to heaven for all eternity.

THE JUDGEMENT FOR UNBELIEVERS

- Unbelievers cannot produce good fruit because they do not follow God's plan.

- The angels will gather everyone who does not produce good fruit and they will be sent to hell.

- Hell is described in unpleasant terms such as: a lake of fire, an unquenchable fire, a place where the worm does not die, and a fiery furnace where there will be weeping and gnashing of teeth.

THE JUDGEMENT FOR AMBASSADORS

- Ambassadors produce good fruit because they follow God's plan.

- The angels will gather everyone who produces good fruit and they will be sent to heaven.

- Heaven, in the gospels, is not described as well as hell.

- Heaven can be assumed to have the following characteristics in contrast to hell: a place where there is God, angels, perfection, and hope.

WORKS

- Unbelievers believe that they can resolve their sin problem by doing good works.

- They hope they can do enough good works to outweigh their sins and earn a place in heaven, however God's judgement does not work like that.

- All God has to see is one sin in your personal record book and he will pronounce you guilty and condemn you to hell.

ETERNAL LIFE

- Eternal life is by grace through faith, not good works.

- Eternal life is a gift because Jesus has done all the work for us when he died on the cross.

- To experience eternal life four things must occur: one must be redeemed, forgiven, be born again, and be baptized in the Holy Spirit.

- Redemption and forgiveness frees a person from judgment and going to hell for all eternity.

- Being born again provides spiritual new life in order to live with God.

- The baptism of the Holy Spirit empowers Ambassadors to work God's plan with power.

REDEMPTION

- The remedy for our sin nature is redemption.

- Our sin nature is the root cause of our problem for committing sins, and causes us to be a slave to sin.

- Redemption occurs because Jesus died on the cross in our place.

- Jesus' death paid the ransom to purchase us out of judgment and eternal punishment in hell.

FORGIVENESS

- The remedy for our sins being recorded in our personal book in heaven is forgiveness.

- Forgiveness occurs because of Jesus' death on the cross.

- All of our sins are taken from our personal book and laid on Jesus.

- Jesus died to pay the price for our sins so that they would be forgiven.

- For those who put their faith in him their personal book is cleared of all sin.

BORN AGAIN

- To be born again is to be regenerated with a new spirit.

- Jesus regenerates us with a new spirit so that we can have fellowship with him.

- Being born again makes it possible for Ambassadors to see God's plan easier when reading from God's word, and helps them to experience a vital relationship with God.

BAPTISM IN THE HOLY SPIRIT

- Jesus is the one who baptizes in the Holy Spirit.

- Jesus said that the baptism in the Holy Spirit would give them the power needed to work God's plan effectively.

COMMITMENT

- Unbelievers must know the commitment that Jesus expects before making a decision to follow him.

- Jesus wants unbelievers to deny themselves and be willing to die for following him.

- Jesus said that whoever wants to save his life will lose it, and whoever loses his life for him will save it.

REPENTANCE

- Repentance is turning from working your own plan to working God's plan.

- For unbelievers working their own plan means working any plan but God's plan, which usually has to do with some self-interest: career, money, hobbies, good works, etc.

- Jesus' first disciples left their businesses to follow him. They believed that he was the Messiah and were willing to repent of their own plan to learn God's plan as taught by Jesus.

- These were hard working men who heard Jesus talk about eternal life, and the need to repent and believe the good news and they decided that that was what they wanted and believed that Jesus knew the plan to get there.

FAITH

- Eternal life is by grace through faith in Jesus.

- The gospel message is that Jesus is the Messiah who died on the cross in our place to deliver unbelievers from sin and hell so that they could have eternal life with God.

- An unbeliever can express their faith in Jesus through prayer. A prayer of faith in Jesus can be as simple as:

Heavenly Father, I believe that your son Jesus is the Messiah who died on the cross in my place so that I may have eternal life with you. I accept your free gift and give my life to you to teach me how to live life according to your plan. Amen.

DISCIPLESHIP

- After accepting Jesus as your Savior and Lord it is very important to obtain a bible, attend a church, and join a discipleship group.

- A discipleship group will help you get to know God's plan and learn how to live it.

- I attend a group which does this and would be glad to introduce you to our group.

ABOUT THE AUTHOR

Richard Charles (Chuck) Brown

I am a Christian layperson who loves to study and teach from the Bible. I have read the Bible many times, and the four gospels countless number of times. I was a team leader in a church evangelism ministry called Discipleship Dynamics, and a Sunday school teacher for new Christians. I have been a trustee of a large Assembly of God church, and I am a meticulous and systematic researcher of the Bible.

I have a Bachelor's in Accounting and eight years' experience as an accountant and auditor, and an Associate's in Manufacturing Engineering Technology with 25 years of experience as a manufacturing planner, and system and data analyst.

www.ingramcontent.com/pod-product-compliance
Lightning Source LLC
Chambersburg PA
CBHW071452040426
42444CB00008B/1299